ONCE UPON A TIME . . . ◆ ◆ ◆

EILEEN COLWELL

M.B.E., F.L.A., DLITT.
Eleanor Farjeon Award

Foreword by Jan Mark

PENNINE PENS

In memory of my dear sister, Vera May Colwell

PREFACE

My thanks are due to my four friends, Catrina Atkins, Mary Durning, Billie Reeves and Eileen Rose who, over the years, deciphered my handwriting after I became partially sighted, and supported me with their advice and encouragement. This book would never have been completed without the help of my friend and editor, Chris Stephenson, who brought order and cohesion to a manuscript which had been written over a number of years.

Thanks also to my many friends for their support and friendship throughout my long life.

FOREWORD

We take so much for granted. I borrowed my first library book, at the age of five, in 1948. Seven years later I had commandeered the whole family's tickets and was borrowing twelve every week. For me, and my generation, there were always books to borrow, always a library to borrow them from. It was one of the three fixed points of my compass; home, school, the library. I took it for granted.

When it was time for Eileen Colwell to leave school in 1920, and choose a career, she wanted work that would bring her into contact with children and books. "Books suggested work in a library, but had that anything to do with children? The answer was probably 'no' . . . " Eileen learned to love books at home. This, her own book, records the dispiriting lack of interest in children's literature, and its readers, that only hardened her resolve, the struggle against indifference and outright hostility to the presence of children in libraries and the providential enlightenment of the councillors in the North London district of Hendon who saw a need and were guided to choose the right person to fill "a part-time, temporary appointment to develop a children's library service".

This must have been one of the longest temporary appointments in history. By the time of her retirement Eileen had been party to all those other things we take for granted now: readings and story-telling sessions, the Schools Library Service, the Youth Libraries Group, the Carnegie and Greenaway medals; every last thing that encourages literacy and then makes it worthwhile, has evolved in part from that first venture in Hendon. On the back of this burgeoning culture the numbers of books published annually for children is now approaching five figures.

"I had become part of that revolution in publishing," Eileen Colwell observes as she surveys, a little dazed, the achievements that surround her. Not so. She was there from the beginning, at the heart of it, one of this country's most influential revolutionaries.

Jan Mark
October 2000

HENDON PUBLIC LIBRARIES

The Magic Casement

W. Burden Evans.

" Infinite riches in a little room."
—*Marlowe.*

THE

QUARTERLY MAGAZINE

OF THE

JUNIOR LIBRARY

THE BURROUGHS   No. 3

N.W.4   September, 1930

A design for the front cover of *The Magic Casement,*
the magazine edited by Eileen Colwell

CONTENTS

There is no substitute for books in the life of a child, and the first understanding of this simple and irrefutable truth must come from his early perception of his parents' faith in it.

Recipe for a magic childhood – **Mary Ellen Chase**

During National Library Week one year, a television personality interviewed borrowers at a library to enquire why people used the service in this day and age. Her random questions brought such answers as: "For information" – mainly on practical subjects; "To borrow records, videos and the like"; "To use the photocopier". A student found the library a convenient place in which to write up his notes. Some young people used it as a meeting place.

"And why do you come to the library, my dear?" she asked a child of nine indifferently.

The child looked at her with disdain. "For BOOKS, of course," she said dismissively, and pushed past her into the junior library department.

All my life has been spent with books and children, an association that has brought me happiness and fulfilment. I never considered any other career, although at that time in the history of libraries, it might well have been thought an impossible dream...

Eileen Colwell

PART ONE
GROWING UP

CHAPTER ONE

All my life I have loved stories that begin 'Once upon a time…' What better beginning could there be for a story, which inevitably – for memory is not infallible – has something of the fantasy in it? What I think I remember may bear little resemblance to what actually happened in what is called 'real life', but the essence of the truth is there, although the hills and valleys are untouched by time. At the end of the long tunnel of my life there is the world of childhood, perhaps recalled more vividly than yesterday.

One fact is indisputable: I was born on the sixteenth of June 1904, in Robin Hood's Bay on the coast of Yorkshire, a village whose romantic name has caused me embarrassment when signing hotel registers abroad. Robin Hood's Bay, a Yorkshire Clovelly, runs steeply down the cliffside with houses at all angles and levels, to a grim shore of black granite slabs. Year by year the cliffs are being eroded and landmarks are disappearing.

But the sea and sky are still as blue as they were when I was a child, the smell of seaweed is still on the wind, the red roofs still tumble away to the sea. Strange to think that this sea and this village were the first things I saw in the world; the wind blowing in from the sea my first intimation of the forces of Nature. Perhaps this early acquaintance with the open sea gave me a perpetual longing for space for my gaze and a liking for a landscape seen from high places.

At the beginning of the century when my father, a Wesleyan minister, came to live here, the village and its people were very much as Leo Walmsley describes them in *Three Fevers*. Inhabited by seafaring men, smuggling had been rife and there were still many connecting cellars and cupboards where forbidden goods such as tobacco, tea and brandy were hidden. These were smuggled in by sea and distributed on ponies across the lonely moors. A romantic setting for someone who later would be so involved with adventure stories for children.

The manse was one of the Victorian villas sprawled at the top of the cliff, 'Up Bank'. The village, with its cobbled alleys and jumble of red pantile roofs, was 'Down Bay'. In winter it was often isolated and frost and snow made the steep-stepped streets impassable. It was not unusual for the sea to sweep into the narrow bay and up the slip to the coastguard's cottage and the village street.

When my father came to this circuit in 1903, he already had two children, a boy and a girl of six and eight. Two more were born during the three years of his ministry here, my younger sister, Vera, the last of the family, and myself. My brother told me that he remembered the arrival of the doctor on horseback, his bag strapped to his saddle, on the June morning when I was born. He probably thought, in those innocent days, that the doctor had brought me in his bag. At the time he was far more interested in a toy cart which was due to arrive at Thorpe Station. This had been ordered from Gamage's catalogue, a treasure that gave us many hours of pleasure as we cut out the pictures of beautiful ladies and gentlemen from its pages. My elder sister, however, welcomed her two little sisters with joy, for she was a motherly soul and continued to mother us for the rest of her life.

It is reputed that our nurse used to push the pram up the steep street beside the two hundred steps to the shore. She thought it no hardship to wheel Vera and me on the way to Whitby along the cliff top. Walking was our only means of transport and we thrived on the fresh air blowing so strongly from the sea and the moors. I must have been a hardy child, for at the age of two and a half I set off alone along the cliff top and was discovered wandering happily at the cliff edge some distance from home.

It was Whitby that gave me my second name, Hilda (a name which I discarded as soon as I became an independent adult), after the famous Abbess who in the 7th century founded a house for monks and nuns – and kept peace between them for twenty-two years! She also, it is said, drove all the snakes of Yorkshire into the sea, a useful feat which must have enhanced her reputation at the time.

Charles Wesley is said to have visited this remote village several times during his travels on horseback throughout England. His local preachers were known as 'Lantern Saints', because it could be midnight before they reached home after a service. In 1779 a chapel was built. It was perched on the hillside so that it had several galleries at odd levels. From one of them, restless children could see the waves beat on the rocks below. There was a three-decker pulpit in which my father, a small man, must have been almost invisible. He provided for this disadvantage, as I remember him doing in other circuits, by standing on a footstool. It was a precarious position and his children sometimes watched apprehensively – even sometimes half-hoping…! In the 19th century there was a landslip which snatched the two or three cottages between the chapel and the cliff top, so that the old building now stands on the edge of the cliff.

Robin Hood's Bay was one of the many places in which we lived as children, for we moved at least once every three years, occasionally more frequently. I discovered as I grew up that the knowledge that one must leave one's friends at the end of the three-year period cast a shadow on making close friendships. Unlike people who live in one neighbourhood all their youth and grow up with friends and relatives, we had no 'roots' and were always 'foreigners'.

Why choose such a life, with its demanding service and its low pay? Primarily, of course, it was – and still is – a vocation, a 'call from God'. Perhaps in my father's case his background had some influence. All his forebears for three generations were strictly nonconformist. Visiting the Wesleyan Burying Ground in Hucclecote, the Gloucestershire village where my great-grandfather, Richard Colwell, worked as a cooper and small farmer, we found the names of eighteen Colwells who had been buried there. At that period, 'Dissenters' were not allowed burial in a Church of England graveyard, nor were their names entered in the Church register.

Of Richard Colwell's twelve children from two marriages, four became Wesleyan preachers, one a local preacher in Gloucester, two sons emigrated to Australia where they became ministers of some note. My grandfather showed such promise as a local preacher that he was persuaded to study for the ministry here. He was much respected for his sincerity and eloquent preaching. He wrote articles for religious magazines and several books for children which such titles as *Pleasant Talks about Jesus* and *Good News for Children*. He died in 1887 at the early age of 45, leaving four sons who all became Methodist ministers, inspired by their father's example and Christian character. Two were well known as Chairmen of their District, in Liverpool and in Manchester. The third son was my father, who went to America for his first years as a minister. The fourth also emigrated to the States where he became a minister, as did his son. The family produced eight Methodist ministers in three continents in a century, but the record has not been maintained by their descendants, though most of the Colwells inherited a gift for public speaking.

My own father, Richard Harold Colwell, began his training for the ministry after a short period as a clerk.   After two years in active service, he came up against the Methodist rule of the time, that a man must serve seven years before marrying, as did Jacob for Rachel.   This my father was not prepared to do, for he had fallen in love with a young woman who worshipped at Finsbury Park Chapel.   Always an impatient man, he resolved to emigrate to the States where conditions were more liberal and humane.   There he gained the degree of Bachelor of Philosophy – always his favourite subject – entered the American ministry and was appointed to his first circuit.   In 1894, my mother went out to marry him.

My mother, Gertrude Weiss Mason, was the eldest of ten children – three girls and seven boys.   The family originally lived in Preston but moved to London where mother's father, Henry Cornwall Mason, set up business as a chemist.   The family were staunch Wesleyan Methodists, active in the local chapel.

All the knowledge I have of my mother comes from a diary I discovered after her death.   This was written in an exercise book and covered the period between 1884 (when she was 17) and 1895, when she joined my father in America.

From entries in her diary, it appears that, like many young women of her time, she was much concerned with the state of her soul.   It is evident, however, that she was also a lively young woman who loved parties and pretty dresses and both male and female friends.   She even confessed that she once smoked a cigarette.   She went on holiday quite often, chiefly to relatives in Derbyshire, Southsea and Newcastle.

She fell in and out of love with visiting preachers and various other religious young men, for she was romantic.   However, these 'love fits', as she called them, never came to anything and were, no doubt, an emotional escape from the narrow life she led as the eldest in a large, not too prosperous, family.   Therefore when her cousin, Marcus Hedley, who had emigrated to the USA, came on a visit in 1880, they 'took a fancy' to one another.   He told her of the plains covered with golden wheat, about the blue mountains and his farm, which appealed to her romantic nature.   Marcus (several years older than she was) vowed that he would come back to England when she was twenty-one and marry her.   He did come back, but although they were much in love, her parents forbade marriage between the cousins.   By this time in her life my mother felt that she could not marry a man who was not 'converted', that spiritual state essential in the Wesleyan belief. Marcus, apparently, had not experienced this. It was at this turning point of her develop-ment that my mother met my father.

What courage it must have taken to travel to America in those days! To leave family and friends, never having been out of England before, to make the long voyage to a strange country, landing in a city that must have been intimidating even in those early days, friendless and with very little money. But my mother was no weakling; she had an independent spirit and was glad, I am sure, to escape from an autocratic mother for a more adventurous life. She and my father were married immediately in New York in a minister's parlour, as was the custom in America, and left for their first home in West Stockbridge, Massachusetts.

Life was difficult for this lonely young wife, for money was short and salary had to be collected personally from members of the congregation – often 'in kind'. My mother records a notable happening in a diary fragment: a 'kind' man had given them a dollar, some honey and two cans of fruit, and promised a sack of potatoes.

Then came the first baby, anticipated with great joy – and it died. After this my mother became more and more unhappy and when a second baby, my elder sister, was born, my parents decided to return to England. They could only afford steerage, the voyage was rough, they were both seasick and my father often had to drive away rats from the sleeping baby at night. In 1897 they were back in England again.

But their hard times were not over, for my father was required to serve another five years as a 'probationer' on a single man's salary. So, with a young child to support, they travelled wherever they were sent, staying for short periods in Keswick, Edinburgh, Mablethorpe (where my brother, Eric, was born), London and Saffron Walden, living in lodg-ings with no settled home of their own. Little wonder if conditions became strained between them.

So they came to Robin Hood's Bay and this, I think, was a happy time in their marriage. After an interval of six years from their return to England, I had been born and my sister Vera arrived in the last year. The family was now complete, life was more settled, my father was writing poetry and articles for Methodist magazines with some success. After a long sojourn in the wilderness, life had promise once more.

And so our stay at this happy and interesting place must come to an end. We must move to what was, to us children, a new and therefore exciting place. To father, too, each new circuit was a challenge and a new area to explore, for he was a great walker. What it meant for my mother is not recorded. She had to face the upheaval of her home and the unknown conditions, with four children, two of them below three years of age, Vera still a baby of five months.

CHAPTER TWO

Our destination was the town of Halifax and nothing could have been a greater contrast to our previous home. Instead of the healthy air from the sea, we now breathed smoke-laden air from the mills. The busy streets were frightening after the quiet village: there were too many people! For my mother, the change was particularly unwelcome, for the house was damp. Fungus grew on the kitchen walls and the wallpaper showed ominous patches, and it wasn't long before all four children had coughs and colds, especially the two youngest.

I remember nothing of this, of course, but my father, justly indignant, insisted that we could not be expected to stay in such conditions with young children. So after only a year we moved on, although my father, with his customary energy, put in hand the finding of another more suitable manse for the next minister.

In 1907 we moved to Rushden in Northamptonshire, a town of blue-slated roofs and harsh Midland brick. The countryside was pleasant enough. It had interesting alleys and streets, along which I was wheeled in my push-chair, a kind of wheeled chair with a velvet seat and head-rest. I remember nothing of the route we took but I can still recall how safe I felt in it with my feet firmly on the foot-rest. The wheels hummed, and so did I, and when the chair was tipped over the edge of the pavement, the jolt made my voice shake in an interesting way. Passing under a bridge it was exciting to sing as loudly as possible.

To this place, too, there belongs a glimpse of childhood, for I know that I didn't like water being poured over my curly head so that the drops ran into my eyes. I protested loudly each time, until, one day, I suddenly lost this dread. I found I could blow bubbles and even sing – about a cow.

I remember little of the house and garden, except a large cherry tree from which my brother obligingly dropped cherries for his sisters – and himself.

Most weeks I went with my mother to the Women's Meeting which she was expected to lead in every circuit. While this meeting went on, I played with other young children on a blanket spread on the floor. When my mother had to leave at the end of the three years she was given a small presentation – she always won the love and respect of 'her women' – and to my astonishment and delight I was given a gift too. I can see it still: a tiny green leather bag and an alphabet book. Round every letter twined a flower in colour; my favourite was the letter P with its wreath of scarlet poppies.

It was here, in an area famous for the manufacture of shoes, that for the first and only time in our lives we had shoes made to measure. An old man, his thumb black with cobblers' wax, came with his tools. We stood on the table on a piece of paper and he drew round our small bare feet with a stub of pencil that tickled our insteps and made us giggle. Those shoes must have been a pleasure for they were *personal* and made of soft, pliable leather.

In 1909 we made our next move, to Bradford-on-Avon, then a sleepy little town. I was of an age to observe and remember, for it was here that I first went to school and became a person, an individual, able to wonder about life and what went on around me. Childhood is the time when we receive impressions and establish the kind of person we are to become. At this time too, Vera, only 15 months younger than me, was to become a companion with whom to play and share pleasures.

Our introduction – that is, Vera's and mine – to Bradford-on-Avon was inauspicious and undignified. The ladies of the congregation took us into the garden where we rushed about excitedly. On being told to be quiet we sat down on the stone wall of the terrace, only to spring up clawing frantically at our frilly knickers and embroidered petticoats – we had sat on a colony of ants and had to be carried away ignominiously, howling with anguish.

Bradford-on-Avon in those days had not been 'discovered'. To us, the great tithe barn of Cotswold slates with its four thick walls and its huge double entrance through which a loaded wagon could be driven, was just an exciting place to play hide-and-seek; it meant nothing to us that it was 800 years old. The small building on the bridge across the river Avon, we believed to have been a prison where a Wesleyan preacher had once been imprisoned. The beautiful arched bridge was a good place from which to watch the river and the boats. Bradford was for us a town where it was fun to live, all up and down, but with meadows and wild flowers in abundance.

A fascinating part of the town was the Shambles, a narrow shopping alley where our grocer had his shop with its brass scales and row of gleaming weights. There was always something to watch, for this was before the days of pre-packing. Everything had to be weighed on the spot – butter, flour, rice, soap-flakes, candles. The sounds were appetizing, the patting and slapping of butter as the grocer attacked it with wooden pats soaked in water, the pattering of rice as it poured on to the metal scales. And what a delicious smell, compounded of apples, oatmeal, tea, cheese, the latter tempting to the Hunca Muncas who lived in every grocer's shop. But what made our mouths water was the sweets. The grocer's son was said to be 'keen' on Dell, our older sister who was now in her teens, and he brought her bags of sugary sweets with loving messages imprinted on them. While we sucked these messages away – we couldn't yet read – my brother would read out the most sentimental ones before eating them, much to the embarrassment of our blushing sister.

Milk was brought to the door in a large churn banded with gleaming brass, and poured out with a ladle so that it foamed into the jug. Each trade had its distinctive badge – a striped apron, a straw hat – which we recognised from our Happy Families card game. We were surprised to discover that the butcher's name was not 'Mr Bones'.

On Sundays we attended the 18th century Wesleyan chapel in the Market Street. Winter and summer we climbed the steep approach and the long flight of steps in our 'Sunday best', wearing woolly gloves which tickled, or silk gloves which squeaked. Once I had a muff to wear, the height of elegance! Sundays were 'special'. We always had a cold dinner so that the maid could go to chapel too. There was no secular reading, such as school tales, but only 'Sunday' books, perhaps from Stead's *Books for the Bairns*, pious tales with titles such as *Meg's Little Children* or *A Peep behind the Scenes*. *Ministering Children* I disliked because of the extreme goodness of the characters. *Froggy's Little Brother* touched our hearts. Games, too, must be suitable for Sunday, but I don't remember being bored by them. We played quite contentedly with our Noah's Ark, or painted Bible pictures and, when we could read, searched out pictures for a Bible clock.

Sometimes on a summer evening, our older brother and sister might be left in charge of us, for we did not go to chapel twice in the day. Then Eric would conduct a service for us and our dolls. He was always the preacher, standing on the seat of a high-backed chair turned back-to-front. His sermons were brief and included much thumping of the upholstery and his text was usually "There shall be weeping and gnashing of teeth". He accompanied this with such gruesome gnashing of his own teeth that we were quite petrified with dread and *our* teeth ached in sympathy. This was followed by the collection to which we contributed a halfpenny, our week's pocket money, on condition it was returned to us.

But our happiest Sunday evenings were when our mother stayed at home with us and we sung hymns round the piano. The gas was turned low and a candle lit on the piano and we sang our favourite hymn

> Jesus bids us shine with a clear pure light,
> Like a little candle burning in the night...

Chapel services were not very enjoyable. The pews were hard and our legs didn't reach the floor. Our pennies for the collection had a habit of escaping from our hot sticky hands and rolling under several pews. My brother would gladly have crawled after them but this sensible behaviour was frowned upon. We sat, one on each side of our mother, her feather boa tickling our cheeks, and the voice of the preacher in too long sermons becoming a drone that was as soporific as lettuces to Peter Rabbit.

In Bradford-on-Avon I experienced the great adventure of going to school, something I had been looking forward to for some time. Nowadays small 'private' schools are often decried as being staffed by ill-trained and incompetent teachers without the paper qualifications that count for so much today and hide a different kind of incompetence. There have always been exceptions to such criticisms and at least in such schools children were individuals and there was the intimacy between staff and children that is only possible in small communities. There was discipline but it was not, in my experience, of a repressive kind and it gave a feeling of security to young children. One knew where one was and what was right and what was wrong, and a child needs help to recognise such distinctions.

My first school was one of this kind. It occupied a tall Victorian house and the staff consisted of Miss Cochran, the head, and her assistant. Miss Cochran was dignified, dressed always in black, very erect. We children thought her very old, but I suspect she was not more than in her forties. She had her rules of conduct which we did not dispute, but she was just and kindly. Her assistant was much younger, tall with her hair in 'bangs' and she always wore a long skirt to her ankles and a long-sleeved blouse.

So one day in September of the year when I was five, almost six, I proudly crossed the road to school. We younger children donned spotless white pinafores. We had no pencil boxes yet so we wrote on slates with squeaky pencils or chalks. We drilled to music holding dumb-bells with small bells on the end, which tinkled pleasantly as we moved our arms in simple exercises. We sat on backless forms, our arms folded behind us so we could sit up straight.

One of my first tests in applied maths was to count the letters of the alphabet. Even at this early age I showed signs of my ineptitude for arithmetic, for I managed a different answer every time I counted and at last gave up in despair.

Reading was different – I don't remember when I learnt to read – and it was easy to rattle off "The cat sat on the mat…" I cannot remember that magical moment as a child when the black characters on the pages of a book took on meaning, but from that moment I became a compul-sive reader. Children's books were not easy to come by in those days but whatever I could beg or borrow, I devoured. The paperbacks of that period to be found in Methodist homes and Sunday Schools were reli-gious in tone and tales of poor children and death beds, but I soon left them behind in favour of my father's library with its classics and even fairy tales and legends on which he based his children's addresses on Sundays. My mother, too, told us stories and recited poetry at times, but she did not altogether approve of my habit of dusting the stairs with an open book in my other hand.

The boys in the school were a nuisance – one would kiss me as I read, absorbed in the book, much to my annoyance. Another, a nasty, weasel-faced boy with a drop on the end of his nose, was fond of swaying the form to and fro with me perched precariously on the end. When I consulted my mother about this she said, "Next time he does it, stand up". So I did, with great success, for the boy and the form crashed to the floor and he was carried off howling with a bump on his head. I watched with satisfaction.

I had a dislike for being kissed, perhaps because, as the minister's child, my round rosy face and curly hair caused the sentimental ladies of the congregation to plague me like this and I was too young to be able to defend myself from such unwelcome attention. Later I adroitly stepped aside at the crucial moment. How many children must dislike this assault on their privacy.

I enjoyed school. To learn was a pleasure and there was good basic teaching at this school, small as it was. How nice to hear words called 'poetry' and to join in repeating "Great wide, wonderful, beau-tiful world…" Everything was new and interesting and now that I could read, a new world of stories was open to me. Already I was a 'bookworm'.

Out of school, there were simple treats. Once a year the fair came to town and pitched its tents in the field not far behind our house. Lying in bed, I could hear the delightful brassy music of the roundabout. It cost a penny to ride on the prancing horses but a fourteen year-old boy who lived next door offered to take me and was infinitely patient with the little six-year-old girl, not minding when she clung to him in delicious terror as the horses whirled dizzily round. (Not many years after, he was to be killed in the First World War.)

On Gunpowder Day there was a bonfire and treacle toffee and frightening fireworks – rockets hissing into the air, Catherine wheels spinning and spitting in many colours, noisy squibs which made us jump. But what bliss to hold sparklers and watch their miniature rain of stars in the dark night.

Then there were the festivities for the accession of George V in 1911. Our rich next-door neighbour, a patriot old gentleman, provided a brake for the Sunday School children and we had a picnic in a farmer's field. Tea was made in a large urn which gave it an interesting metal flavour, and we were each given a paper bag which contained a bun, a jam tart and a cake. After this, we ran races between two cow pats. I can't remember ever winning anything, but we manse children did our best.

One expedition was the annual outing for my mother's Women's Meeting. Each member paid a small sum a week (at one time, one penny!) into a fund and then, on a summer day, everyone piled into an open brake drawn by two clopping horses for an excursion to some beauty spot such as Westbury White Horse. If there was a steep hill the younger ones got out to save the horse. We were allowed to go on this outing and considered it a great treat. They were days of delight, the fresh air, the quiet country roads with plenty of dust but no cars, the unusual sensation of riding behind horses; the picnic when hungry and excited, our ham and egg pie tasted like nectar. Then the thrill of climbing to the White Horse, sitting on its eye – there was room for fourteen people. On the drive home in the evening light, everyone tired in a pleasant way, we all sang hymns and the songs of the period. One worrying time, my mother had had to accompany us in a pony and trap because the brakes were overcrowded. At ten o'clock at night she hadn't returned, to our great alarm. The pony had fallen dead in the shafts and a local farmer had rescued Mother and brought her home! But such drama was rare.

One outing I remember particularly for its strangeness. My father took me to the grounds of a 'stately home' where a fete was being held. There I saw what was called an 'aerial railway'. One end of a rope was fixed in a tall tree, the other end was much lower. For a penny, customers could travel down this line at some speed holding on to a pulley. For some reason this man I watched – in amazement and some dread - was wearing a lion's head! Did lions walk about wearing only their heads? Then my father took me to peer round a canvas screen behind which was a small one-seater plane. "Look well!" he said. "Some day there will be many of these machines flying in the sky!" I looked up into the empty blue sky with wonder – but I could not really connect this jumble of struts and canvas with flying like a bird, although I accepted such marvels without question in the fairy tales I loved.

One of our greatest pleasures was to be taken along the country lanes – then safe for children and dogs – in the trap our brother had made for us from a packing-case. It was mounted on wheels, had padded seats and bowled along at a fine rate, with my brother between the shafts. He often teased us but was the kindest of brothers always, although he was embarrassed if his pals caught sight of him with us. He took us to gather primroses and cowslips along Rowdy Lane, and would wade into marshy ground to pick wild yellow irises for our mother. Our faithful companion on such expeditions was always our beloved mongrel Jack, a fox terrier of sorts.

Down one side of our garden was a high privet hedge and sometimes a hand would appear above it with a gift of strawberries or vegetables. It was our neighbour, Mr Long, a kind old man who would invite us into his house and allow us to play bagatelle, although I had to stand on a footstool to reach the table. When I first read *Little Women*, I at once imagined Mr Lawrence to be like our old friend with his bushy eyebrows and white beard and kind ways.

Our greatest delight, however, was our dolls and with them we had all kinds of imaginative adventures, using them in stories I had read, sending them on journeys and dressing them in different ways with the help of our elder sister. Dell and Eric made us a fine dolls' house for Christmas and a dolls' school the next year, complete with tiny books and maps, a family of children and even a teacher and a school bell. My brother was the carpenter, my sister the seamstress and never were presents more appreciated. Our most acceptable presents were doll-sized furniture and fittings for the house and school and doll stories have always fascinated me. Surely dolls are some of the best toys for young children even in these sophisticated days, for they offer such a scope for imaginative adventure. Alas! modern dolls come complete with expensive wardrobes, leaving no scope for the designing of clothes and the adventures which go with them.

I suppose we could be considered deprived children nowadays, for our toys were few and mostly home-made. Then there were the season-able games – skipping, hopscotch, hoops, tops which we carefully cray-oned so that when they were whipped they became whirling things of beauty. For wet days there were transfers and, most wonderful of all, Japanese flowers, tiny dried up scraps which when floated in water opened magically into delicate blossoms. We played simple card games like Snap and Happy Families, but never with playing cards, which were considered sinful. This lack of sophisticated games involved us in hours of inventive construction and busyness, making use of whatever materials we could find about the house or in our mother's 'Piece-bag'. For me, books were a necessity from an early age and I looked forward eagerly to the 'new book' I should always receive on my birthday or at Christmas. We were seldom bored or idle.

Like all children in Edwardian times, we suffered from too many clothes. Long stockings, many buttons, including boots which required a button-hook and were difficult to manage alone. Our clothes were embroidered and frilled but at least they were feminine and it was possible to tell the sex of a child from any angle! How we should have appreciated the freedom of modern clothes however, and they would have made our mother's life much easier, for there must have been endless starching and ironing to keep us looking fresh and cared-for. Washing day was a ceremony involving boiling clothes in the copper, sheets flapping in the breeze, the smell of freshly-ironed clothes and the iron heating on the fire.

Our weekly pocket money was a halfpenny at this time, later raised to the generous heights of a penny. Looking back, it is astonishing what we could buy for this: 'hundreds and thousands', chocolate drops and toffees. For penniless days there was the silver teapot on the sideboard which always had a secret store of ABC biscuits with a coloured dab of some sweet stuff on top. Adults could sometimes be prevailed upon to provide a little cocoa and sugar in a saucer which was delicious on a licked finger. There were green gooseberries in the garden and sticks of rhubarb, which at that age we enjoyed chewing, a snack, the very thought of which now sets my teeth on edge. Everything possible was tasted and smelled – the senses were all important as a source of pleasure.

There was infinite wonder and interest in the world of small creatures, and in flowers which grew close to the ground and which the adults were too tall and pre-occupied to notice. My favourite was a field of buttercups golden in the warm sun; if I knelt in the grass amongst them I was in a secret world.   We children would gaze absorbedly as we held a buttercup under each other's chin, seeking from its golden reflection to see whether we liked butter.   There were primroses – is there any scent so delicious and evocative? – wild violets with their elusive scent, harebells and windflowers so fragile I scarcely dare touch them.

And so to bed with the glimmer of the popping gas jets for company. As I gazed at them half asleep, it seemed to me that the walls of the room receded into infinity and, terror-stricken, I would close my eyes to shut out the boundless space between me and safety.   Only sleep could rescue me.   I thought of this experience as being 'far away' and it troubled me for years.   I don't think I ever spoke of it to adults.

Our early childhood was a happy one, with loving parents and an elder brother and sister to whom we could turn for support and affection.   As they were six and eight years older than us respectively, we seemed very young to them and I think they regarded us as a kind of responsibility.   This affection and protective relationship with us, continued to the end of their lives.

CHAPTER THREE

Wherever we lived, we knew that we should have to move in three years' time, possibly less. Our destination – unless our father had a previous invitation – was decided by some mysterious process known as the 'drafts' drawn up by the Methodist Conference Stationing Committee. There were three of these and it was not until the third was issued that we could be quite sure of our new home. Great was the excitement as my father consulted the atlas and *Everyman's Encyclopaedia* for information about the new environment. Sometimes there would be a protest before the final draft – on one occasion we were put down for the Shetland Isles. We children were all in favour of such a move (we could see ourselves riding about on Shetland ponies), but our unromantic parents decided against it as there was our education to be considered. Today Methodist ministers can stay in one circuit for at least six years – how my mother would have welcomed this. Not perhaps my father, for the itinerant ministry appealed to his restless spirit and meant that there was new country to explore.

Our next move was to the other end of England, to Chester-le-Street in Durham. This meant a long journey by train for sick children. No wonder we arrived looking pale. The circuit steward who met us exclaimed at our wan appearance. "A-way, hinny! We'll soon put some colour into your cheeks. The South hasn't good air like we have here." It is true that Wiltshire is inclined to be enervating, very different from the harsh invigorating air of the Northern counties.

At Chester-le-Street we were in a mining area instead of an agricultural one. As we drove down the main street, colliers were squatting on their heels in doorways, against walls, a typical posture for men who spent much of their time in cramped conditions down the mine. A little boy ran beside the cab wearing nothing but a red waistcoat – we two little ones considered him very 'rude'.

The new manse was on a hill leading out of town. It was the usual four-square building, rather like a child's drawing. Its condition rather dismayed our mother for the previous incumbent, a retired missionary, had a Creole wife and her ideas of housekeeping were not my mother's. Hens had been kept in the boxroom, leaving traces of their stay, and there was scribbling on the wallpaper over what was to be my bed. (Sometimes we found traces of the children who had lived in 'our' house before us – a lead soldier on a ledge, a little note signed 'Leslie Lob'.) The house had been given a hasty clean by the ladies of the circuit but it was not very inviting. New decorations were promised apologetically. We children longed to explore the garden but first we must take tea with the ladies of the church. This was a lavish meal but our long journey had not left us with much appetite. We knew we must be on our best behaviour, for this was the first meeting in the new circuit and the impression made mattered.

At last tea was over and we were free to rush into the garden. Was there a swing? There was! Somewhere to play, useful bushes and corners where we could hide! To our joy, the garden was quite large with a vegetable plot – much neglected – a lawn and a slope down which we later learnt to ride a bicycle.

Inside the house there was the usual furniture, often cast-offs from wealthy Methodists – horsehair sofas which prickled the back of our knees, heavy sideboards, shabby carpets, unlovely wallpapers with faded squares where the last minister had hung his pictures. No labour-saving devices. A range in the kitchen which had to be black-leaded, a steel fender which must be kept shining, a copper in the scullery for washing. In those days the itinerant clergy had no furniture of their own beyond a piano perhaps and some bric-a-brac. Household linen and china were provided by the circuit, but all self-respecting wives would have some linen of their own of good quality and a best tea-set. The household linen was often threadbare and it was hard to renew it from the meagre allowance made quarterly by the church.

The familiar pictures - the 'Monarch of the Glen', the family portraits - were hung on the walls and the ornaments were put in place, the marble clock given to my grandfather, the mandarin whose head nodded if anyone trod heavily across the room, the large shell in which you could hear the sea, the doorstop which was a lump of green crystallised glass in which beautiful flowers were imprisoned, the vase of fresh flowers which my mother always gathered. In the evening we gathered together as a family, we two small girls in our special chairs which just fitted us, our dolls on our laps, the cat curled up on the basket chair, the rest busy sewing or reading round the large dining room table covered with the green serge cloth fringed with bobbles. This was home again and we were safe.

Chester-le-Street was an interesting place. From our windows we could look across open land to Lambton Castle, the seat of the Earls of

Durham.   My brother worked on this estate to learn practical forestry. We could almost see a second castle, Lumley Castle, ancestral home of the Earls of Scarborough, a castle dating in parts from the 13th century. When I was first taken on a visit to this I thought it was just like my fairy tales.   There was a legend about it that appealed to my romantic heart. It was said that the castle was haunted by a beautiful ghost called the Lily of Lumley who drowned herself in the castle well because she wasn't allowed to marry her true love.   She had a habit of appearing, dressed in grey, and then disappearing through a wall several feet thick. As I listened to the story, I looked through a narrow casement window into the heart of a wood, the ground hidden in a mist of bluebells.

Lambton too had its legends, a very famous one of this 'loathly Lambton Worm' and the witch's curse which doomed the heirs of the estate to die always out of their beds.   The earl who had the courage to kill the Worm was the first to suffer and so did five others of the nine who inherited the estate.

Chester-le-Street was once a place of legend and history, dating back to Roman times as its name indicates, but by Defoe's time it was described as "an old dirty thoroughfare town", its origins long forgotten.   It had associations with Saint Cuthbert too, for the monks of Lindisfarne in the 9th century halted here in their long search for a resting place for the saint's bones.   It was one hundred years before the saint found sanctuary in Durham Cathedral.

There was a reminder of the Middle Ages in the Shrove Tuesday Football Match between the upper and lower town.   It is reputed that the original ball was the head of a Scotsman!   The violent battle between the townsmen was still waged when we were in Chester-le-Street.   All the shops were boarded up and peaceable citizens stayed indoors.   The ball usually ended up in the burn to terminate the violence.

But history did not concern us very much.   Chester-le-Street was just another place to love and we were more interested in its possibilities for play than its activities in the dim past.   At one side of our new home was a long strip of unused garden where my parents decided to keep hens.   We liked the fussy hens, but the belligerent cock was a different matter.   If we ventured near him he would run at us and peck our bare legs while we fled with squeals of dismay to our refuge, a house made out of a packing case in which our piano travelled in each move.   Our brother obligingly made us a little window in this so that when we sat inside, we could look out with one eye through minute curtains.   No grown-up ever disturbed us if we retired there, it was our secret hiding-place, a necessity for children. My mother was a wise woman for she gave us much freedom in which to enjoy our childhood. We each had our 'chores' but, these done, were free to play.

Eric had his own farmyard, tiny bantams. He would crouch by their run, one or two of the tiny creatures perched on his head or shoulders and chirrup softly to them. Our pets were a cat and our dog, Jack, bought expressly to cure we two younger ones of our unreasoning fear of dogs. Nobody could be afraid of Jack and he was our faithful companion throughout his long life. He travelled with us everywhere and had a seaside holiday as we did.

Our life in Chester-le-Street revolved round two main problems, education and the outbreak of war. It was now 1912 and I was eight, Vera six, my older sister and brother sixteen and fourteen respectively.

It was decided that we should be educated at home by a governess. My elder sister had already left school to help at home, my brother would soon be leaving the grammar school for he was not academic and hoped to have an outdoor life. The local elementary school was considered unsuitable for we younger children. I don't think it occurred to the members of the congregation to criticise my father for this. Ministers' children would be expected to be a little different. Snobbish? Perhaps, but the local elementary school of that period, especially in a mining area, was very different in character and accommodation from the primary school of today which most ministers' children would attend as a matter of course.

A governess in a middle class home like ours was considered one of the family, and while she was paid little – it is a mystery looking back how my parents afforded any salary at all – she was not expected to do more than look after Vera and me. Ours was a busy household and my mother had duties in the church. She also trained children to give concerts in aid of the church and the National Children's Home. All these activities meant she and my elder sister had little time to spare for us, although we were in no sense deprived of love.

Our first governess was an emotional and neurotic Welshwoman. She taught us well but we suffered under her tantrums of jealousy, for she resented anyone who shared our affection. This included my elder sister who had mothered us since her childhood, so there was constant friction between them. My poor mother was the mediator and was treated to the governess' hysterical fits of weeping and complaints of the way in which she was being treated in this 'Christian' home. On one occasion I heard one of these outbursts and Miss G say dramatically,

"Look at the handkerchiefs soaked by my tears". I quite expected to see a dozen of them in a bucket and was much disappointed when I found only one. For a time this situation was endured for the sake of our education, but things became worse and worse. Every lesson we had with Miss G deteriorated into vituperative remarks about our sister and our father. We were a little afraid of this violent woman who was so full of twisted jealousy. "You will not tell anyone what I say!" she commanded with flashing eyes which seemed to bore through us. We didn't, but one day I let slip some remark which gave away the truth. I was questioned and told all. Soon after Miss G departed suddenly and we relaxed into the customary peace of home.

Our next governess was very different, a real 'old maid', gentle and retiring, a gentlewoman in manners but with a singular lack of knowledge of anything that might be useful to her pupils. She had come with a warm recommendation from someone who probably hadn't the heart to speak the truth in case the unfortunate woman might not get another post – she had no resources. After two or three days in which she spent the evening being instructed by my sister as to what to teach us next day, the teaching was handed over to Dell and Miss R amiably helped in the house.

Our new 'teacher' was determined we should be diligent and a credit to her, for Dell had an aptitude for teaching and organisation which was frustrated by her life at home. Being our sister we could not pull the wool over her eyes by pleading tiredness or lack of ability. We had to work really hard and enjoyed lessons by heart; and, occasionally, we were able to persuade her that we ought to learn how to cook, which made a delightful and satisfying interlude, for we were able to eat what we cooked. Fortunately, she always rescued our efforts from the oven before they were burnt to cinders. Cakes took so long to cook that we felt we might as well spend the waiting time playing in the garden. Of *course* we would remember to come back in time – but we hardly ever did.

At last a young woman was found who really was qualified to teach us, was not at all neurotic and was young enough to become my sister's friend. She was always known to us privately as 'Polly Ann' and we loved her. She was large and fair and, in my memory, always wore a green velvet blouse crossed by a gold chain on which was a gold watch. She taught us music, watched to see that we did our practice and took us out for a walk every day, rain or shine. It must have been tedious for her at times to be so much in the company of two small girls, but she was always willing to join in with our games and fun, throwing a ball, bowling a hoop, finding flowers (classed as 'Nature Study'). I have vivid memory of walking along with her as we all three sang hilariously

> There was a man called Michael Finnigan
> He grew whiskers on his chinnegan.
> The wind came out and blew them in again,
> Poor old Michael Finnigan,
> Begin agin...

...*ad infinitum*. We had a good grounding in the 'three Rs' and other necessary subjects for our age, and found we could keep up with other children when we went to 'proper' school in our next circuit. Polly Ann was one of the family and I like to think she was happy with us.

One less formal part of my education was invaluable for my future choice of career. My father, always a bookman, delighted to see my growing love of reading, planned a novel way of encouraging my budding taste in literature. He ordered a number of titles from Nelson's Sixpenny Classics – yes, sixpence a volume, with hard covers too – and had them stored at a local newsagent. Each fortnight he took me there to 'choose' a book to read. My 'free choice' was really controlled by his pre-selection, of course, but it was free enough to delight me and I looked forward to my fortnightly treat with excitement. So I sampled Dickens, Scott, R.L. Stevenson, Charles Reade and a host of authors as well as the children's classics – *Alice in Wonderland*, *Little Women* and others. By the time I was eleven, I had a fair knowledge of 'good literature'. Of course, there was much in the books I did not yet understand, but I took from them as much as I was ready for and returned to them when I was mature because I had not been forced to read them as a 'task'. This solid foundation of literature formed a basis on which to build when I had to evaluate books for children and adults in later life. This I owe to my father and am eternally grateful for his wisdom.

Of course, I read other books as well: my brother's adventure tales, my sister's romantic stories, her *Girls' Own Paper*, my younger sister's annuals. Once, a bound volume of the *Strand* came our way and, oh, what treasure I found there – E. Nesbit and Conan Doyle (I still remember the fearsome illustrations to his creepy *The Speckled Band*) amongst others. Charlotte M. Yonge was a favourite author of the time with her pious heroes and heroines, as in *The Daisy Chain*. I read everything that came my way, good, bad and indifferent, and I am sure the

29

best way to encourage children to enjoy books is to turn them loose on a wide selection of books and leave them to find those that matter to them. The result of such freedom of choice may not be what adults want, but for the reader it opens the door to a lifetime of solace and enjoyment.

One of the chief activities outside the home was to support my mother in bazaars and concerts at the chapel. It was her duty to be the prime organiser of such affairs and we were expected to back her loyally – and usually did. So we embroidered pinafores, made artificial flowers from crepe paper, and created useless pincushions. Our cane baskets were really practical and well-made, however. My mother made what we considered to be really *beautiful* hat-pins from sealing wax, with glittering streaks of gold. These were much in demand for the unwieldy hats of the period. We helped on stalls, managed Bran Tubs, Lucky Dips and were peripatetic sweet sellers, selling (and occasionally surreptitiously sampling) our wares for a penny or two.

My mother trained innumerable children in what were called 'Action Songs'. As we had much experience of these, we had to take part in them. Dressed as flowers or waves in costumes made from crepe paper, we led the songs importantly. I still remember the words of Mrs Ormiston Chant's song:

> See the waves are tossing
> Far out to sea,
> While to and fro the great ships go,
> Whate'er their course may be.
> Thunder of billow and spray   (*Much stamping of
> infant feet*)
> But following fast on their way
> Are some so tiny they whisper sweet
> As they come with a whisper right up to my feet...
> (*Graceful retreat of charming manse children as they hold
> their frilly dresses above their
> tiny feet*)

Our elder brother and sister too, had to suffer for the cause. Fortunately they both had good voices and so sang duets:

> Pretty Betty don't fail
> Let me carry your pail

30

> Safe home to your cot in the dale,
> To hear the fond tale
> Of the sweet nightingale,
> As she sings in the valley below-ho-ho,
> As she sings in the valley below

Their tuneful renderings of folk songs or popular ballads were much admired.

Occasionally, as a treat, we went by tram to Newcastle where there was a marvellous emporium called The Penny Bazaar. Everything really was a penny; so we were able to buy all our Christmas presents for the rest of the family. Small notebooks, pencils, useful articles of all kinds, were to be found in tempting profusion, but it was a worrying decision to make with our limited funds.

Just once we were taken to see Sanger's Circus when it was in the neighbourhood and sat entranced at the clown's antics and the beautiful ladies riding on the backs of prancing horses. Compared with this delight the visit of two evangelists was disappointing, although this too was in a large marquee and the well-loved hymns and choruses of Moody and Sankey ('Tell me the old, old story;' 'Jesus wants me for a sunbeam,' etc.) were quite enjoyable. I remembered another evangelist who visited our chapel at this time. He was called Josiah Nicks, a venerable man with a flowing white beard, who patted us on the head and murmured, "Two immortal jewels for His crown", which made us feel very important and sanctified.

Holidays were always at the seaside. We set off with a hamper of food and linen, we four children, our parents and the dog, Jack. Our greatest trial was that, arriving on Saturday evening, the waste of Sunday lay between us and the sands, for we were not allowed to play there before the secular Monday arrived. Seaside landladies were usually kind but the holiday was not much of one for my mother as she still had to cater and shop for the family meals each day.

On the beach, my father put up the square tent with its umbrella roof so that we could dress in our bathing costumes with decency. And it *was* dressing too, for we wore costumes made of stout material in navy blue trimmed with braid. Dell had to wear a skirt over this garment to blot out her figure even more discreetly. These costumes when wet were most uncomfortable, heavy with water and difficult to dry. After this 'treat' came the welcome pleasure of drying ourselves with sandy towels and then having our 'elevenses' while my mother relaxed in her deck chair.

31

There were no amusement centres, few ice creams; sometimes there was a row of donkeys on whose back we could ride sedately if we had enough money. The holiday was a kaleidoscope of rock pools, coloured shells, seaweed and briny smells, long lazy days on the sands or wide ranging walks with my restless father while my mother enjoyed her well-earned rest in the sunshine – it was always sunny, of course.

The last year of our stay at Chester-le-Street was the first year of the Great War and this meant that our house was often full of soldiers from a nearby camp. They came for meals and baths and the feeling of home our parents made for them. We loved them, for they were always kind to us small fry and played with us and brought us little treats. They sang and whistled and flirted with our sister so that she fell in and out of love with the younger ones. The married ones sometimes brought their wives who would stay overnight with us and make the meeting longer. Two soldiers I remember particularly, one a Scottish sergeant whose wife became our lifelong friend, the other a young lieutenant, sensitive and unhappy, who found the army discipline harsh. He came from a cultured home in an old manor house (which we were invited to visit later). Both these young men, like so many others, were killed within the year.

But the war only became real to us when our brother was old enough to be called up. He had tried to enlist before he was of age and had been sent home ignominiously, but now he really became a soldier, a private at first, then a lieutenant. We all missed him for he had a great sense of fun and was unfailingly kind to us, although he loved to tease. It was my mother to whom his absence was the greatest grief, for she knew well he might never return and he was her only son. Every day there were lists of casualties lost in battle or 'missing'. Eric went off cheerfully for, like most young men of the period, he wanted to do his part and no doubt thought of it as an adventure.

It was at Chester-le-Street that I had two strange and almost mystical experiences. I was about ten years old. We were walking along the river bank one spring day with our governess and, while she and Vera were sitting down to rest, I wandered away. Almost hidden in the bushes I found a gate and going through it came to a solitary magical world. On one side was a steep bank fringed with red campion flowers and the deeply flowing river, on the other a wood clothed in the vivid green of Spring. It was utterly still and solitary. Then I saw, between the trees, a sea of bluebells, so vividly blue that my eyes were dazzled and I closed them and stood enchanted in a moment of ecstasy that has remained with me all my life.

The second experience was equally strange and intense. One Summer day when I was alone I was suddenly conscious of a chord of music. It seemed to come from the air around me and stretched up into the cloudless sky, a perfect harmony of sound, a grandeur of music. I forgot everything as I listened and slowly it died away into a throbbing silence. Years later when I first heard Addison's hymn 'Spacious Firmament on High,' this experience came back to me. This then was 'the music of the spheres…'

But, war or not, the time came for us to move on. The usual routine began, the numerous packing cases were brought in from the shed where they had been stored since the last move, the sitting room was cleared, the carpet taken up and packing began. The packing cases were a source of pleasure for we younger ones, for round them and in them we played all kinds of imaginative games. Meanwhile my mother continued her meticulous packing, for it was her proud claim that she had never had anything broken in her many moves. Everything was packed in newspaper saved during our three years stay – no removers to take over and clear cupboards. The members of our family have been renowned for neatly and safely packing parcels ever since, a lesson learnt in our early days. Finally, the cases were fastened, labels written and tacked on and we were ready to go. Once the packing cases had been despatched, my mother would begin to clean the house from top to bottom so that it would be in order for the next minister. My father meanwhile had packed his books, a long drawn out task, for it meant he had to look into books he had forgotten, and tidied up the garden ready for someone else's crops – or neglect.

CHAPTER FOUR

On our train journeys to other circuits we were pretty sure to meet other ministers' families who were also on the move, for we always moved on the same day, the Thursday before the first Sunday in September. At junctions, my parents would often come across friends known in other circuits and this was a pleasure. Fortunately for us – we were not good travellers – we usually had a reserved compartment to accommodate the six of us, plus our maid who might be travelling with us to see if she would 'like' the new district, and our dog and cat. This time we were going to a place called Rawmarsh, near Rotherham, an industrial area.

However, the manse was behind the chapel, not on the busy road. Our garden, dropped steeply to a valley, and looked over rolling country. Gales swept over the landscape without any hindrance. Indeed on one New Year's Eve, so noisy was the wind that we younger children were frightened to go to bed, so were allowed to stay up later than usual. It was fortunate that this was so for the wind blew in the large windows of our bedroom and scattered sharp spears of glass across our beds. On the next New Year's Eve the high wall which prevented our garden from plunging into the valley was blown over, leaving a dangerous precipitous drop. No wonder a strong wind fills me with apprehension even today.

The exciting part of this move was that now we were to go to a 'real' school, a High School for Girls at Rotherham. I was just eleven, and my sister nine. This was a great adventure for us because, until now, we had had a rather sheltered life - with an older sister or a governess to accompany us wherever we went. Now we had to walk down the hill where the clanging trams ran. From there we travelled on a rattling tram to a spot from which we could cut across country, cross a bridge over a canal, beside which were two or three cottages, then walk through a residential area to school.

What a thrill it was to wear school uniform for the first time: a green tunic with a bright golden-yellow girdle. In the Summer we had the added elegance of a hard straw hat known as a 'straw benjy'. I had read about such joys in school stories by Angela Brazil and it seemed, according to such books, that all kinds of exciting things happened at school – midnight feasts, spies, underground passages and exiled princesses. School turned out to be sadly disappointing in this respect, but it had compensations of other kinds. The girls were friendly, the staff not too bad and the headmistress was rather sweet, small and dumpy, bespectacled and kind, not at all like the awesome headmistresses I had read about. I enjoyed learning, except for arithmetic, and there were new subjects to interest me, French, Housewifery, Science - with fascinating equipment like bunsen burners, and litmus paper which turned colour in some mysterious fashion. We made beautiful crystals and nasty smells, but it was all done in groups so there was an air of excitement and rivalry which was pleasant. Geography wasn't bad for I liked making neat maps and, anyway, I had actually been to quite a number of places in England. Art was more ambitious than the 'blob' painting I had executed with the governess. Games now expanded into hockey which, while rather painful at times and connected in my mind with a running nose and cold extremities, was good fun, for both Vera and I could run fast and so were given positions where this was useful. I even played in a cricket match once, much against my will, because no one else was available. There was a cheer when I, as wicket-keeper, caught a ball: it jumped off the bails and hit me violently under the chin so that it fell into my hands; I would much preferred to have missed it. Tennis was only for the older girls.

French, at this stage, was enjoyable for I was elated to be chosen for a minute part as a dwarf in *Snow White*. My two lines were recited in what I am sure was execrable French for, while we were all well grounded in grammar, we had no proficiency in *spoken French*. Singing too was enjoyable for I liked music, although I cannot imagine it gave much pleasure to the mistress to hear us thundering "O who will o'er the downs so free" or "Bonnie Dundee".

'Domestic Science', that grand title for very ordinary skills, I found boring (it has remained so!). We learnt painfully to make a pair of cotton knickers with gathers which we stroked with a pin, a horrible exercise which sets my teeth on edge even to think of. Needlework was not my strong point and tended to produce a grimy unfinished article at the end of the term. Washing and ironing I liked better and before I left school I had been promoted to polish linen serviettes with a 'glossing' iron – (It had a rounded bottom and was very heavy). My other acquaintance with cooking – then and for most of my life since – was to join a line of girls wearing aprons and dusters round their heads and to sweep in turn the spotless flue of the cooking range which was never lighted. Possibly the cookery course came to the point of cooking something edible in time, but I had moved on before this happened.

My great cross was Arithmetic, due I think from hindsight, not only to a natural lack of ability but also to the teachers I happened to encounter, who had little patience with a dullard like me and could not understand my complete lack of comprehension about sums which involved trains meeting and passing at certain speeds, or bath water running into various receptacles at X gallons a minute. Why bother with such hypothetical matters? And why in Geometry spend hours proving a line was straight when one had only to take a ruler to test it? Such matters seemed to me unimportant and anyway my mind went blank when faced with an impatient teacher who used the unfair weapon of sarcasm.

But English was the subject I enjoyed most. To hear poetry read aloud, to be encouraged to read new kinds of books, to become aware, to my surprise, that I had read much more widely than most of the other girls was encouraging to my diffidence in this unfamiliar world of school and competitiveness. Often at playtime I told stories to the youngest children from lower forms, for I had read so many fairy tales that I never lacked for material and could invent any details I had forgotten. Perhaps the children who gathered round me for these few moments found school life rather frightening and felt more secure listening to the old stories. In these formative years also because of the War, there was a shortage of paper and text books and of teachers.

Food was short too, for rationing was not as well organised as in the Second World War. In our case meat was a problem, for the butcher had a way of cutting us short because he was sure a 'gentleman' like my father would not attack him as did some of the frustrated women who had large families to cater for. The flour became so bad and had so much potato flour mixed with it that the resulting home-made loaf was grey and heavy. On one occasion my elder sister wept when she saw the result of her baking for the family: grey, heavy and dingy. It was diffi-cult for my mother to provide any kind of balanced diet and we were quite excited if some unexpected bonus of food came our way from a farmer or friend. Much time was spent in queuing for necessities and if word got round that a particular shop had a consignment of meat or fats, a queue would gather mysteriously in a few minutes. Somehow we were usually far down it – perhaps we were not good at pushing!

Unlike the Second War, there was little danger from the air, but we did have one Zeppelin raid, aimed probably at the iron works. During the night we were awakened by the rumbling of the heavy machine over the town. My mother took Vera into her bed, but, as I made no sound, thought me asleep. I wasn't, but, for some reason of pride culled from my latest adventure story or because I disliked making a 'fuss', I pretended to be oblivious. I am sure I was really much afraid. I was certainly comforted to hear my mother's steady voice reciting the familiar words of the 23rd Psalm as the Zeppelin passed over with menacing roar.

Meanwhile the routine of life in the manse went on. Each day was opened with family prayer led by my father who read a short passage from the Bible and made an extempore prayer, simple prayers we could understand – if we listened. The family – and the maid – obediently knelt down, with elbows on a chair and posteriors in the air. Sometimes I counted the buttons in the upholstery, sometimes I stroked our dog as it passed close to me. I don't remember that we ever rebelled openly against this ritual; later it lapsed as circumstances altered. Perhaps it was not such a bad preparation for a busy day. We had of course to say our prayers at night also, calling down blessings on our relatives and anyone else who appealed to our wandering minds.

Sunday School should have been a 'must' for the minister's family. Strangely enough, we managed to avoid it in some circuits. I don't know how my parents justified it. (We chose to go when we were little because of the attractive 'holy' pictures which we won by attending and collected jealously.) Sunday Schools included, as was natural, little boys who behaved badly and tweaked our curls or pigtails, but I don't think this was the reason for our non-attendance. It was related that in one assembly, the teacher, discoursing on the theme of 'God is Love', turned suddenly to a naughty boy and said "Hold tha' tongue or I'll clout yer!"

The Band of Hope, run by the temperance societies, was a favourite source of entertainment, for sometimes there was a magic lantern show. The colour, the jerkily moving figures as the slides were changed, delighted us. True the pictures were usually of the sad fate of nasty men who drank and landed their families in the workhouse, but just occasionally a humane official would slip in a funny series just to amuse us. We sang songs with catchy tunes with great vigour –

> God bless our youthful band
> Oh, may we firmly stand,
> True to our pledge...

I knew what a 'pledge' was, for as the minister's child, I cheerfully signed the pledge to abstain from intoxicating liquor many times before I was eleven. We learnt too that 'The best side of the public house is the outside,' so I hurried past such buildings, wondering what untold horrors lurked inside.

As we grew older we were expected to remember the preacher's text. When my father preached, we were often embarrassed for he was something of an orator and waved his arms about and became excited in a way we considered let us down. However, his children's addresses were always interesting and ingenious and he usually had something new to show us, a nail, a ball, a piece of string. What was he going to make of these; we wondered, but we were never disappointed, for it was always interesting. The singing of the hymns was usually enjoyed by everyone. Methodism was born in song for Methodists enjoy singing each other to Heaven. Repeats in lines in the good old Methodist tunes went with a 'go', and to hear a congregation singing Watts' great hymn 'I'll praise my Maker while I've got breath...' full blast, is an experience. The organ was sometimes disconcerting, wheezing or dying out with a wail or refusing to play at all because the boy who pumped it had fallen asleep during the sermon. My mother made a mysterious remark about the choir sometimes, saying that it was maybe true "if the Devil was anywhere, he was in the choir". I saw a great many ornate hats on the women's heads but I couldn't see anyone like the Devil, at which I was rather relieved.

Of course, we entered for all Scripture examinations, and were expected to do well, for "if the minister's children did not know their Bible, how could other children be expected to either?" When we won prizes, however, it was sometimes remarked darkly that of course we were in a privileged position.

My father was above all a conscientious visitor of his flock and sometimes I would go with him. I would sit with him in someone's 'parlour' waiting for the housewife we were visiting to 'redd herself up'. The room was always very quiet for it was seldom used. Everything wore antimacassars; on the table would be the family Bible; on the walls, family portraits stared stiffly from dark frames. Aspidistras or geraniums locked out what light there was and there was a smell of furniture polish. The only sound would be the heavy tick of the grandfather clock and if we spoke, we did so in a whisper.

We were not always welcome. I remember well visiting a remote farm to which we had walked. Through the window, as we waited to be admitted, we could see a table set for tea, with eggcups for boiled eggs. Alas, the eggcups were whisked away before we were asked in. But sometimes even I was welcome. In one house the one room was littered with children of diminishing ages. In the midst sat a cheerful miner in his shirt sleeves, playing the concertina. His *eighteenth* child was about to be born. "I'll call her after yon little lass," he said cheerfully, smiling kindly. I felt quite proud.

Sometimes, if there was room I went with my father in the 'Gospel Chariot', a horse and trap which carried him and a local preacher to their appointments in distant villages to which there was no transport. Congregations at these small places were small, perhaps only a dozen, but there was a homeliness and friendliness about these isolated people and their sincerity was so obvious that even I, a child, could feel a happiness there. After the service we would be the guests of some farmer to a gargantuan meal and I would be taken to see round the farm by some reluctant girl of whom I was as shy as she was of me.

My brother was now at the Front as a second lieutenant and the only news we had of him was one of the laconic field postcards which at least assured us he was alive. His good looks and friendly nature and his pleasant tenor voice made him a favourite with his fellow officers and his men. On a route march, out would come his mouth organ, which he played well, and he would start some song which his men could join and feel more able to swing along, tired as they were.

We were all anxious at the frightening reports of losses in battle and all too often it was the young officers, scarcely more than boys, who were killed. When Eric came home on leave from the Front, we would realise something of the strain he was under and the terrible conditions in which the men fought, above all the mud. He told us little, but our parents must have guessed how precarious life was.

One day a field postcard arrived addressed to me. This was unusual but when I read it I realised why Eric had done this. Dell was now away from home, in a post in a Harrogate school, so I was now the eldest at home and I must help my mother all I could. My brother was wounded and being invalided home. Soon he was in a military hospital in Manchester and my parents were able to go and see him. He had a bullet through his arm and his leg was shattered. It had been badly set and had to be rebroken and set again and was slightly crooked for the rest of his life. He was to be in hospital for over a year before he was fit enough to resume normal life. The story of how his life was saved was one of the innumerable acts of courage which went unrecognised by any award. He had been leading his men to the attack when he was hit in the leg and fell. As he lay helpless, a bullet went across his chest and through his upper arm, causing such extensive bleeding that he became unconscious. But his batman had seen him fall and with the help of another man (who was killed) he dragged my brother, under fire, to a place from which he could be picked up by an ambulance. Eric did his best to get a VC for him but, as an inconspicuous lieutenant, he had not enough influence. However, he kept in touch with him all his life and was able to help him in difficulties. Eric had a strong sense of duty and love of his country. When the Second World War came, he volunteered again and, though too old for active service, served as a major in the Pioneer Corps and acted for the rest of his life as a welfare officer to his men, much loved and respected by them.

So three rather dreary years, overshadowed by war, came to an end. My life at school had been happy enough for I was interested in all manner of things and read omnivorously. The country round Rawmarsh was not exciting but we could walk and we two had our small-size bicycle which we shared, riding in turn. On long walks with Vera and her friends, I would tell interminable stories, a blend of what I had read and what I invented.

Now came our last move as a family, to Penistone near Sheffield. My father preached for the last time and everyone joined in the traditional hymn for such occasions 'God be with you till we meet again', sung slowly and with mournful relish that brought tears to the eyes of the more susceptible. But I think we all knew that most of those present were already looking forward to a 'new' minister, and that we ourselves were already thinking of our new home.

Penistone was reputed to be the coldest station in England; however this did not concern us for, our luggage going by rail, we were travelling by more unconventional means. As Penistone was only about 15 miles from Rawmarsh, we were driven in an open landau. My parents sat facing the horses; my sister, the maid and I, opposite them. Vera nursed the cat, our dog sat on my feet. We were packed round with personal luggage and last minute things; bunches of flowers from members of the congregation were on the folded hood and a group of people from the church and idle spectators waved us goodbye or looked on curiously. As we drove along behind a pair of horses, people turned to stare and to wonder whether we were a cross between a wedding party (but why two children already?) and an outing. We passed through villages, usually mining communities, and children ran by the side of the carriage shouting and laughing. We had no largesse to throw, we could only wave.

Another stage in our lives was beginning, one that was to break up our family disastrously and to bring much pain to us all – and maturity to me.

CHAPTER FIVE

Penistone, a small town on the edge of moorland, was a more interesting and congenial part of the country than industrial Rawmarsh. In spite of our unconventional arrival there, we were made very welcome at the new manse, especially by a neighbour, a girl a little older than myself who became a lifelong friend. We had scarcely settled in when she came with another friend to welcome us and tell us about our new school. These two girls were so lively and confident that I felt shy and unsure of myself.

At this time an education other than that of the state schools had to be paid for privately unless a scholarship to a grammar school could be won. We children never qualified for these grants and *all* the expenses for education had to be paid for from my father's meagre salary. I can only guess at the sacrifices that were necessary. No one expected help from the state but, on the other hand, prices were reasonable stable and income tax low. Life for the housewife was hard and there were no labour-saving devices in the home, so help in the house was necessary. It was expected of the middle classes that they should hire domestic help, and indeed this was one of the few openings available for women to earn their living. No one considered it menial to work for someone else, and maids and 'Nannies' were often family friends. Until this move, we had always had a maid and we children loved to visit her in the kitchen and play games and help her make 'rag' rugs. Most of the maids we had were good-living and pleasant young woman - although in Chester-le-Street it was discovered that the maid of that time had been taking me to a house where I was entertained by a friendly woman while the maid herself was occupied in a rather different way with the son of the house. But this behaviour was an exception and we experienced nothing but kindness from our girls, and on the whole I think they were happy in our family.

One disadvantage Penistone had for us was a garden full of docks. My father had insisted that these must be cleared before we arrived, but they had been scythed down only and lay in heaps which housed multitudes of earwigs. For months my poor mother would shudder as she picked up a saucepan and earwigs fell out of the handle. So widespread were the pests that we children - for the first time in our lives - were allowed to say our prayers in bed, for if we knelt earwigs might crawl up our bare legs. We took care that this concession should last a long time, for the lino was cold and hard and the bedrooms were always arctic in temperature.

Now life was to begin again for we must go to a new school, a local grammar school within walking distance – but only just. This part of school life would be doubly important for me because during the next three years I must take the qualifying examination we called 'Matric' and decide what I wanted to choose as a career.

So, almost at once, 'set books' appeared on the horizon, usually guaranteed to destroy any feeling for them as literature for life. I was fortunate for R.L.Stevenson's *Travels with a Donkey* and Lamb's *Essays* were two of my books and I loved them – and still read them. (What delightful phrases R.L.S. used – "He prooted mellifluously like a sucking dove," for instance!) I discovered poetry, too, from the new *Poems of Today* and began to realise that poetry is not so much the thing said as the way of saying it. History I already found fascinating, although my lack of ability for 'Maths' precluded me from remembering any dates. When I took the Matriculation History paper, I quoted one date only, that of the Battle of Sudan, and this I remembered only because it was associated in my mind with a fine sounding sentence about Napoleon III: "This was the culmination of his folly and humiliation..." which I used in my paper with satisfaction. Science had no place for girls in this school, so I must study Botany from scratch and achieve the necessary standard in two years – not helped by the fact that in the exam we were given *mignonette* to dissect and draw! Out of school we had music lessons and, thanks to our governess' perseverance in making us practice, we had become fairly good pianists.

So in 1920 I sat for Matriculation (I was 16 by a week or two) as a trial run and passed in all subjects except – easily predictable – Maths, for this subject was now hopelessly beyond me. However, I won the School Cup for "H'English", as the bluff Yorkshireman who presented it called it, which comforted me for my failure elsewhere.

Very soon after we moved to Penistone the War came to an end and – officially – life returned to normal; but it was a very different normality. 1914 had been the end of an era, a time when there was some feeling of permanency and security, set against a background which had changed little in a century. Each individual had a clearly defined place in the social order, but this class distinction was unified by a common code of behaviour and belief. An ambitious and able man could change his social class, as my own grandfather had proved by rising from his working class to the professional status of a minister of religion. He had achieved this by hard work and intelligence, and a conviction that he was called to serve God in this way.

In 1919 the aftermath of the War in Europe became real for the insular English, for the distress amongst the children of Germany and Austria could not be ignored. My mother read of the starving children and saw the appeal in *The Times* by the newly-formed Save the Children Fund, for a home for a year for a child. My parents made what cannot have been an easy decision financially, to foster a child in this way. Members of the church offered to give practical help and our neighbour also agreed to foster a child, so that the two girls could be company for each other and a link with home.

So one Winter's evening my mother brought 'our child' home to us. Her name was Sidonie Dammerer and she came from Vienna. She was ten years old and her only words of English were "Good night" and "Thank you", which she used impartially in answer to every question. She wore out-grown clothes which my mother found to be miracles of careful darning and patching, for she obviously came from a good and loving home, a child spared with much heartache.

Sidi became a loved member of the household and shared in everything we did. She was allowed to attend school with us free, but had to start in the kindergarten, tall as she was, because of her lack of English. She soon learnt to communicate for she heard nothing but English spoken, except for the times she spent with our neighbour's foster child. I hope she was happy with us – the poor child was often homesick – but we kept her in touch with her parents through the year. When she went home, she was completely fitted out with new clothes by the help of kind people. We did not lose touch with her – she grew into a beautiful girl and married a landowner in Yugoslavia. But after the Second World War we could discover no trace of her although we tried through many agencies. We could only conclude that disaster must have overtaken her, for we felt sure that she would have tried to contact us too had she been alive.

During our time in Penistone, my brother had been demobbed and with his War Gratuity to back him up, he had taken a course in Forestry at Edinburgh University. Now he had a reason to study, he worked hard and successfully for he had the added incentive of falling in love. His fiancee was an attractive girl he had met years ago when we were on holiday from Chester-le-Street. He had lost touch but when he was in Harrogate Hospital recovering from his wounds, he enlisted my sister's help to trace her for he had never forgotten her. He wrote to her, they met and fell mutually in love. This romantic story greatly pleased my adolescent fancy and our future sister-in-law fulfilled all our expectations for she was pretty and lively and accepted us as we did her without reservation.

Adolescence had come upon me but I don't remember it troubling me unduly except that I was occasionally given to floods of tears at the most unsuitable moments - at a picnic, for instance. I was ashamed of this behaviour but seemed unable to help it. Wisely, my parents ignored my lachrymose state as far as possible and I got over it. I had too much else to think about for I must decide on a career, if possible before I took my final exam.

What would I like to be? I was quite definite as to was I was *not* going to be: not a teacher, nor a secretary, or anything domestic, the accepted careers open to women at that time. What I wanted was work which would bring me into contact with children and with books.

Why children? From an early age my sisters and I, as 'daughters of the manse', were required to get on with people, to accept them as individuals in their own right. As we travelled about England, we met all kinds of people in our home and at the chapel affairs in which we were expected to take part. As I matured, I realised that I had an especial concern for children and knew that it was with them I wanted to work - but never as a teacher.

Books suggested work in a library, but had that anything to do with children? The answer was probably 'no', for children were seldom welcome in libraries and my own experience had been depressing. I had belonged to a library in Parkgate near Rotherham. It was 'closed access'; that is, borrowers could not walk about amongst the shelves and choose a book but must consult a book by number. An irascible old gentleman with beetling eyebrows peered out from a gap in the large screen, called an 'Indicator', and listened to my timid requests with a forbidding air. The book I wanted seemed to be invariably unobtainable and this tried his patience sorely, although it was scarcely my fault! At last he snapped "Take this!" I looked at the book he had given me, it was called *Mrs Haliburton's Troubles* by Mrs Henry Wood and was about the troubles of a clergyman's wife. I was ten years old...

But this rebuff, and my feeling of disappointment, had sowed a seed in my mind which I now remembered again. Why shouldn't I – some day – be in charge of a room in a library where children would be *welcome* and be able to choose books they really wanted to read? There seemed little prospect of such a dream ever coming true in my limited experience of libraries, but I was young and optimistic. So my father, my champion in anything to do with books, made enquiries and discovered that there was a college course in London for Librarianship. If I could qualify for a grant, I might be able to attend this. There was no mention in the prospectus of training in library work for children but, once a member of the profession, who knows what might happen? So an application was made to the West Riding of Yorkshire for a grant.

One day I was summoned to the County Hall in Wakefield. A pile of books was placed before me and I was told to select what I thought worthy to be on library shelves, which were 'literature'. An odd way of testing my eligibility for a grant, but an easy one for me for here my wide reading came into its own. I knew without a doubt which were the really worthwhile books, and why, and could pick out the 'classics' approved by adults. After this I was ushered into a large room with a wide semicircular table, round which sat the impressive-looking people who could make my career possible if they chose. I felt even smaller than I was as I sat on the edge of a chair and waited for the questions.

Somehow I made a favourable impression and was granted a Women's County Major Scholarship, the first ever given in Yorkshire for a career in Librarianship. What is more, the amount was increased, so that I need not stay with relatives in London but could gain wider experience of life in a hostel of some kind. I was most thankful for this for I had not wanted to have to live with my grandmother and aunt – I wanted to live with young people and 'go places'.

Now I was to take Matriculation again with the knowledge that I *must* pass at the required standard for on it depended my career and my future. It was not helpful that I developed jaundice just at the time of the exam. I created some interest by my striking yellow complexion and each session was a struggle with my feeling of emptiness and muzziness. I was driven to school each day to save my strength but I managed to sit every paper, and pass them too. After this, to win the 'H' English' cup for the second time filled me with such elation that I dropped it on the way home, leaving a dent as my hallmark. However, my euphoria was soon deflated when I was 'promoted' to the trigonometry class presided over by the irascible Headmaster. I cannot imagine who recommended such a course! I can still hear the despair in the headmaster's voice as he said "Eileen Colwell, leave this class – and don't let me see you again. You will *never* learn trigonometry!" I was intensely relieved to hear it and had difficulty in refraining from dancing out of the classroom.

This phase of strain in my life was not helped by the knowledge which was being thrust upon me more and more insistently that all was not well between my parents.

My father had always been a difficult man, impatient, restless, full of ideas which were seldom successful, and with theological views that often upset conventional Methodists – although his faith in God was unwavering. He had a keen intellect for which there was little scope in the kind of circuit he travelled. I have often thought since that he would have been much happier and more in his rightful sphere as a tutor in a theological college. He was a scholar by nature, had considerable oratorical ability and was keenly interested in young students. As it was, he was frustrated and his ideas seldom came to fruition for want of backing. He invented a new system of shorthand which he used himself but had no money to launch it; he wrote poetry and several books on theology which were never published.

My mother was a deeply spiritual woman but more conventional in her views and she could not accept my father's thinking. She was beloved by the people she met in our circuits and was indeed more popular than my father, which did not help their relationship.

Added to this there was always anxiety about money. Occasionally my father was driven to borrow small sums in order to keep his head above water and this caused him to reproach my mother for imagined over-spending. We were never in debt for long, for this he would never countenance.

My parents' relationship was becoming more and more strained. They no longer understood each other and their life together had become insupportable. As time passed the gap grew wider between them and at times it was very evident how unhappy my mother was. This caused family loyalties to be confused and my brother when he came home, did not disguise his bitterness against his father. I was old enough to realise what was happening, so much so that when, one Sunday morning as she and I were preparing lunch, my mother said "I have something I must tell you", I answered at once, "I know..." At that moment – I was sixteen – I grew up.

There was a chasm between my parents which could never be bridged. It had been growing wider each year, but for our sake they had kept on as well as they could. But when we left Penistone, it was the end of our family life.

Now that Eric and Dell were independent - he at Edinburgh University taking a Forestry course, she working at a school in

Harrogate - and I was moving away, the unhappy affair could be ended. My mother and father parted, never to meet again or to have any communication with each other.

It is not for me to pass judgement – I loved both my parents and did my best to show this for the rest of their lives. I am still convinced that the break up of a family must always cause distress and psychological harm to the children of the marriage, despite modern day acceptance of such situations.

My mother had to shoulder the responsibility of providing a home for herself and my sister Vera. My father would only give my mother a nominal allowance, but she was determined to find work of some kind to supplement this. Not an easy task for a woman of fifty-four, whose only training was as a minister's wife!

PART TWO
TRAINING

CHAPTER SIX

"What *is* Learning...A thing *Rabbit* knows!"
– THE HOUSE AT POOH CORNER

One autumn day in 1921, my mother went with me to University College to register for the course in Librarianship. I was just seventeen, my hair was 'up' in a precarious bun and my face was round and rosy. No wonder that my appearance, added to my small stature, took the official by surprise. Calling my mother aside, he asked solicitously, "Is she really seventeen, and do you think she will be all right alone in London?" My mother assured him that suitable accommodation had been found for me and that although I looked young, she had every faith in my commonsense and ability to look after myself.

It had been difficult to find anywhere for me to board, for the university hostels were too expensive. However, we had heard of a Methodist hostel in North London which provided inexpensive accommodation for Methodist young people away from home. There were about seventeen residents of both sexes, a matron in charge and a visiting chaplain to look after the souls of the residents.

My mother was anxious to see where I was to live so accompanied me to the hostel. When I walked in, the other inmates (I was told later) viewed me with dismay. "What, schoolgirls now!" they exclaimed, for I looked little more and was easily the youngest resident.

The hostel, in spite of the spartan conditions and bedroom space that would be condemned now, was to prove a happy place for me. I, who had lead a sheltered life in a country town and had had little contact with the opposite sex, found myself in a society where everything was discussed, a world of many conflicting opinions. Now I was able to explore a great city, to visit theatres and museums, to enjoy sharing all these experiences with a friendly group of young people. I was soon accepted, in spite of my youth, as someone who did not expect special consideration and could take teasing. We did not dream of using

Christian names, but got round this by adopting nicknames. Not unexpectedly as the youngest and smallest, I was 'Tot'.

The atmosphere was homely. We sat together in our leisure time, had breakfast and evening meal together and, when the meal had been cleared away, the students amongst us settled down round an immense table to study for three or four hours, enlivened by the click of bones of the skeleton owned by the medical students.

The residents whom I grew up to know so well, were an interesting mixture. There were medical students, a dentist, an embryo lawyer, a confidential secretary to a director of companies, who was to advise me on any financial problem for the rest of her life. There were music students, a middle-aged teacher of the deaf who mothered the younger residents and could be counted on to steal down and open the door if anyone wanted to stay out beyond the stipulated hour of eleven o'clock. Not only were there the settled residents but a shifting population of young people who were up in London to attend interviews or take exams.

Into this heterogeneous society I, raw girl from the country, was plunged to face not only these friendly people, but the life of the university with its new subjects. Also I knew that my settled home life was over and, particularly worrying, my younger sister and my mother had an even more uncertain future. It was a prospect to daunt any girl of seventeen perhaps, but I was naturally optimistic and I soon settled into a routine which was my salvation.

In our free time, we wandered round London, explored Kew Gardens and Epping Forest and the parks, or queued in turn for seats in the 'gods' to see Gilbert and Sullivan or to attend a concert at the Royal Albert Hall, for two of our number were in the Royal Choral Society. On Sundays we were expected to help out at the Methodist mission church in Clerkenwell and to attend at least one service. During the week I was useful to play the harmonium for a group of girls for whom we had organised a weekly class. When we walked home from this through Clerkenwell, our girls hurled stones at our ankles to show their appreciation. Alternatively they shied orange peel at me while I played the organ. It seemed that our seed fell on stony ground, but later we discovered to our surprise that several girls remembered us with affection. After all, teenage girls who spent their days sewing buttons on cards needed some outlet for their energy!

An alternative for me on Sunday evenings - often wet in my memory, so that we had to pull the black tarpaulin over our knees on the top of the bus - was to go with a medical student to a Medical Mission in East London.   Here again I played the harmonium for choruses, perched on a small platform.   The front-line children played a weekly game with me.   They would gradually pull the leg of my stool nearer and nearer to the edge of the platform, hoping, gloatingly, that I would crash over-board before the end of the choruses.   Sometimes the singers suddenly quickened their tempo or ceased altogether as I felt my seat dangerously near the edge, and all the time the children sang with enthusiasm: "I've put my name down for a palace and crown".   I had to use pedals to pump air for my playing, so I usually managed to hook my feet securely enough to keep my balance.   These children were a lively, undisciplined lot, poorly clothed, sometimes barefoot, usually dirty – the smell of the assembled company was indescribable – but they loved singing.

Another of my activities was to travel down the Mile End Road to the Fern Street School Settlement, or the Farthing Mission as it was known affectionately.   It had acquired this name because every Saturday morning an arch was erected in the street and every child small enough to pass beneath it was given a small bundle of oddments beloved of chil-dren in those days – a pencil, a notebook, scraps of coloured ribbon, toys - in return for one farthing.   At this mission I helped with the library, a small collection of dog-eared books in a corner of the room, loved by the children, perhaps as a warm refuge from the streets. Many of my clients had bare feet, few were adequately clothed, but they were lively and talkative.   My particular favourite was a cheeky small boy called Kitchener Spicer.

Much of my time was spent on study, of course, and this was hard work, for I had to take all the Library Science subjects – Cataloguing, Classification, Bibliography, Library Organisation, Palaeography, as well as a great deal of English Literature and Latin and French.   Very little work was done in French lectures but they were fun.   Students from all faculties attended to listen to the sarcastic, entertaining Frenchman, Monsieur Stefan.   Fortunately, I was fairly proficient in French so I was able to listen and laugh with the others.   Latin was a different matter for I had never studied it before.

We were fortunate in that we shared the Arts Degree course for Literature and so gained a wide knowledge of the subject from fine teachers.   Then there were our own Librarianship seminars, for which I wrote a paper on fairy tales and myths – I had not forgotten my ultimate intention to work with children.   Each student had to complete a comprehensive book list of their own choice.   I chose children's books.

The only instruction I ever received on work with children was one lecture from Berwick Sayers, that likeable pioneer in the provision of a children's library room. His lecture was a landmark for me, and he remained a friend and encouraging mentor until his death.

The course that I took was the first full-time one to be set up in the country. It was for two years and successful candidates were awarded the Diploma of Librarianship. It was, I think, a good course and syllabus, with a strong basis of literature which, after all, should be our stock in trade as librarians. Our lecturers were outstanding men, for instance Arundell Esidaile, Hilary Jenkins and Berwick Sayers. Being part of London University, the course had the advantage of the wider curriculum and contact with students outside our specific field of Library Science. This was a new departure in 1921. We could take advantage of visiting speakers to the university – in this way I heard Walter de la Mare deliver a witty, hypnotic lecture in his soft almost inaudible voice. There were concerts to attend and our own library functions. I have a vivid and amusing memory of the elephantine Arundell Esidaile, leaping clumsily after a balloon at one of our get-togethers. My entertainments had to be free for I could not ask for more money from my parents, who were hard put to it to make ends meet. (In fact, my mother, now in her fifties, had to find work to support herself and Vera.) But I found interesting things to do; I visited Professor Petrie's department with friends, for instance, and gazed in awe at his archaeological finds, his Egyptian artefacts and mummies. I enjoyed life.

The college 'rags' were not for me. They were usually centred round the college mascot, known as Phineas, a wooden figure that stood outside a shop in Tottenham Court Road. One morning we found that every naked statue in the front courtyard had been painted blue and yellow, the colours of the East London College. This was the day for a ceremonial visit from Princess Mary and her husband. I couldn't help remembering Lewis Carroll's verse:

> If seven maids with seven mops
> Swept it for half a year,
> Do you suppose, the Walrus said,
> That they could get it clear?

More than seven maids set to work with scrubbing brushes but the statuary still had a bluish tinge when the Royal visitors arrived. On another occasion, a large board appeared overnight outside the Provost's office – ELEPHANT ALES SOLD HERE. WALK RIGHT IN. After these escapades, the presence of "any gentleman concerned with the recent disturbance" was requested in the Botanical Theatre. Usually the 'gentlemen' did attend and paid up for any damage they had done. Surely a civilised way to treat students' high spirits.

It was inevitable with a group of young people of opposite sexes in close proximity every day, that there should be some romantic attachments. I was not exempt from this. My first experience was when I noticed a Welsh student gazing soulfully at me. This did not excite any response from me except surprise. He told me that I had "Celtic eyes" (what were those? I wondered, looking with curiosity into the mirror). But when he took me out to tea and hoped that "some day" I would pour tea for him in "our own home", I became thoroughly alarmed; things were moving too fast for me and I was too young and immature to have any consideration for his feelings. I had no wish to pour tea for him either now or in the future, especially as he was intending to be a Methodist minister and I knew what that would mean. Later he emigrated to America and became a fiery Welsh evangelist, so I had a lucky escape.

My next encounter was very different, a young man several years older than I was, who had been a lieutenant in the War. He was a lonely young man, very disturbed by his War experiences and I can only suppose that my fresh young innocence appealed to him. He sent me my first love letter, written on the back of a Euston Railway handbill, which seemed to me most romantic. About to go on my long vacation, we wrote long letters to each other on all kinds of subjects. I like writing letters! But I realised after a time that I was not really in love and could not meet his emotional needs.

Shortly afterwards I found someone with whom I might have developed a lasting relationship. We were thrown much together by our age and similar interests, especially music, for he played the violin and I accompanied him on the piano. He was kind and gentle and a little out of his element because he and his family had only recently left South Africa. It seemed natural to be together and make excursions to theatres. I considered he should not spend his father's money on me. After this ultimatum, I was dismayed to find that he circumvented this ban by doing without his lunch for some days. One play we went to see was Flecker's *Hassan*, an emotional experience for two young and impressionable people. That summer was a memorable experience for us for our romantic matron arranged for us to have an early breakfast, so that we could walk to college together. Ah, those halcyon Summer mornings. We walked along the busy unromantic streets, Pentonville Road to King's Cross and Gower Street - quite a walk! At University College we parted, watched benevolently by the porter.

Why did I end this affair too? Looking back, I realised that the break-up on my parents' marriage had left me with a distrust of marriage and its continuity, so that I was afraid of committing myself to what could turn out to be a mistake. Also I had a feeling of responsibility for my mother and sister – I felt I must contribute to their livelihood as soon as I possibly could. Unlike my fairy tales we did not live happily ever after, for I ended it and never felt more miserable in my life. I never saw him again.

I never regret never having married. I have had the kind of life and experiences that would have left no time for the commitment and duties of marriage. Had I married my life would have been very different. Richer in some ways – yes, but less stimulating for me as a person. I should have enjoyed children of my own, but I have had great joy from other people's children without the responsibility of being their mother.

The time had now come for the final examinations, which I passed successfully in all subjects except Latin, in which I was 'referred'. This was not surprising as I had had to start from scratch and the statutory 'mensa...a table...' Now I must decide what was the best course. I opted to stay in London for a third year as my grant was continued. I felt I should need this length of time to come up to standard in Latin and I could make myself proficient in my knowledge of children's books, visit libraries – and maybe find a part-time job to earn a little money? I hired a typewriter and bought a manual and began to teach myself typing, an invaluable asset throughout my life. I walked everywhere, learning more about London and its environs, visiting museums and art galleries as long as they were free. It was a lonely time, for my particular friends had moved on and everyone was out during the day at the hostel, so I often had the whole house to myself. Sometimes I went to see my stately grandmother at Finsbury Park. She had lost her husband in middle life and had settled down to widowhood for the rest of her life. She always dressed in black with a spotless lace cap on her white hair, and put her grandchildren to shame with her erect carriage. I had another aunt, greatly loved, at Isleworth and went to visit her and her large family when I could afford it and felt I was not imposing on her. Here I found the homely affectionate atmosphere which I missed so much.

54

In the Winter, I was offered a job for three months as a temporary assistant in a branch of Fulham Library. I took it without hesitation, for here was an opportunity to earn a little money for the first time and to repay a little to my mother. The branch was not an attractive one, rather gloomy with a balcony round the main lending department and a children's library in the basement with no natural lighting. The room was approached by a flight of steps down which the children came leaping with loud whoops and clattering of boots. As I was known to be interested in children, I was kindly allowed to take over this department, thus giving the rest of the staff a welcome reprieve. This was not quite what I had dreamed of, but it was a beginning. I had a hard time in that noisy, airless room, but in spite of everything I wasn't too unhappy or inadequate and I found I could command some sort of order.

At that time, library assistants had to suffer an arrangement of working hours which could not have been more awkward. Twice a week I had to work a 'split' timetable; that is, I was free from one o'clock to five but in that time had to have both lunch and tea. As I was a long way from the hostel and the journey required two buses, I could not possibly go back for the afternoon. The only alternative was to walk about – and it was winter – or stay in the library, which seemed pointless unless I had some Latin preparation to do. I decided to go to the cinema sometimes, for it was warm and restful there and provided entertainment. Matinees were half-price and not crowded, so that was no problem. But, because I must be back by five and had a short bus journey, I could never stay to the end of the 'big' picture. Week after week I had to rush away leaving the heroine or the hero in peril or the lovers still estranged. It was most frustrating! Never again in my life did I see so many films, nor wish to, but at the time I blessed this haven from the cold and dreariness of unknown streets.

What a thrill it was to come home at Christmas – home was now in a village near Barrow-in-Furness, where my mother and sister had taken a small business to support themselves – and to be able to take presents bought by my own money. It was worth all the hard work and the discomfort of long bus journeys in all kinds of weather and the 'hotted-up' meals I had had to rely on late at night.

The years came to an end and I passed the Latin exam. I had to find a post somewhere and it would not be easy, for many libraries were prejudiced against these 'college folks' who had no practical experience and were 'snooty' and unwilling to do the menial tasks. Remember that the course I had taken was very new and that most librarians earned their qualifications by attending evening classes or by correspondence courses. This was a considerable hardship, considering the long hours worked at that time.

However, I was young and optimistic, so I wrote to twenty-five libraries offering my valuable services. Looking back, what cheek I had! Most of the libraries did not trouble to reply. While I was waiting for an offer, I spent my summer vacations as usual at a Christian Endeavour Holiday Home in Wales where my elder sister was matron, working on the staff for my keep as a voluntary helper. This was something I enjoyed, for the home was at Conway, with beautiful surroundings and the staff and guests were good company and fun.

In the last vacation I was offered one job at least. It was in the David Copperfield Library in London. The salary was almost non-existent so I had to refuse, for I would not be able to keep myself on such a sum in London and I *must* be self-supporting. I was sorry I could not be associated with such an imaginative venture, for this library was unique. It was situated in Johnson Street, which Dickens had occupied from 1824-28. In its narrow passages and steep stairs, Dickens had set the Micawber family and their lodger Traddles and Mrs Cratchitt had boiled her Christmas pudding, "a speckled cannon-ball", in the copper in the scullery.

Such a house was scarcely suitable for a library, but it was here in 1921 that an American clergyman, John Brett-Langstaff, sometime head of Magdalen House, Oakley Square, established a library for the poor and crippled children of the neighbourhood, Somers Town, in memory of Dickens' own unhappy childhood. It was stocked with books and pictures given by authors and artists, and of course there were books by Dickens and about him.

But to the children of the neighbourhood this was a haven, a treasure house. They queued for hours, even in the rain, for the privilege of spending a few hours in this cheerful house with its bright curtains and miniature furniture and stock of books and magazines, even though every child must first submit to a wash and put on a linen smock. Even 'Babies' were admitted and played in a 'Fairy Dungeon' under the care of a motherly child called the 'Warder', assisted by a 'Fairy' and a 'Giant'. All books had to be read on the premises and not one book was stolen in the years the library was open, a record that puts to shame the borrowers of today. Those in charge showed a sound knowledge of child psychology for they gave responsibility to as many children as possible. Thus twenty boys and girls were 'Staff'. 'Doorknocker' kept a stern lookout for boys who dared to lift the brass knocker out of season; the 'Master of Keys' and his assistant 'Watchkey' were responsible for an enormous bunch of keys (although the same key unlocked every door in the house!). The 'Master of Robes' handed out the smocks and the 'Master of Books' kept order. Then there were visiting adults – the Historian, the Poet, the Storyteller. At nine o'clock all children except the 'Staff' had to go home, the rooms were tidied, the books were replaced and the 'Staff' sat round the fire talking and singing, accompanied on mouth organs.

On one occasion, children from an American Children's Home sent a wreath for Dickens' grave. Two stalwart boys carried a small cripple boy, a 'Tiny Tim', to Westminster Abbey where the wreath was placed in Poets' Corner. After the ceremony, the boys were treated to plum cake by the Dean of Westminster.

This imaginative provision for needy children was handed over to the Borough of St Pancras when the founder was no longer able to look after it. Sadly, it was pulled down in 1934 and its place taken by a block of flats, even the name of the street being changed so that all association with Dickens was lost.

Many years later, I found that one of the head teachers in my own borough had known this library when he was a boy. "It was a place where you could read and no one interrupted you," he said, "and it was there I learnt to love Dickens' books. I still do…"

Just when I was despairing of getting a job, I had a letter from a Lancashire town about a post as senior assistant, at a salary of £80 a year. Even at the time this was a low salary; however I had no option but to accept it. I had the sense to realise that it would be infinitely easier to find a better post if I had 'my foot in the door' and had some practical experience.

So in September 1924, aged twenty, I set out to take up my first permanent position in a library. This was not a children's library of course – that was for the future – but at least there would be children using the library and maybe I could have some contact with them. Perhaps I could even find an opportunity to tell them stories?

>Round the next corner and in the next street,
>Adventure lies waiting for you…

Maybe it would for me.

CHAPTER SEVEN

As I travelled from my home (now in Barrow-in-Furness) to Bolton, my first post, my heart sank. The landscape became more and more industrial, there were few trees and those that I saw were blackened and twisted with the prevailing wind. Mill chimneys stood black against a grey sky. I was coming to a Lancashire town where I knew no one, to strange lodgings and an unknown library. But it was a beginning and I was grateful for that. I had my foot in the door and should not always be in this one library. I must look upon it as a stepping stone to something more congenial and akin to my dream.

The cheery welcome of the porter at the station with his "Here you are, luv," raised my spirits. Lodgings had been found for me in a quiet street of terraced houses with a lady called Mrs Shaw, a widow dressed always in black. She was a little suspicious of me at first but always kind, and she fed me so well that I became even more round-faced while I was in her care. I was given a cooked breakfast, a hot meal in the middle of the day and a 'high' tea and all this only cost me twenty-five shillings a week. As my net salary was only about twenty-eight shillings, this was just as well. The library was a tram ride from my lodgings so I could not often walk. The house had no garden, only a strip of grass in front and a yard behind, but the open country was very near.

When I started work the next morning, I found I was to be senior assistant in nominal charge of the Fiction library on the ground floor. The Non-fiction library was upstairs, in the care of a more experienced assistant and haunted by two 'Dusters' in black overalls who moved slowly round the shelves seizing every opportunity to whisper and giggle together in the corner. The whole of their working life was spent in this unrewarding occupation. As soon as they accomplished one revolution of the shelves, they began at the beginning.

I was not viewed with delight by the other members of the staff, many of whom had never worked anywhere except in their native town. They assumed that, as a college person, I knew nothing at all that was useful, and yet would consider myself superior. I certainly had very little experience of the practical side of affairs. I could understand their feelings at having a young inexperienced woman of only twenty put over them, but surely no one could be envious of my meagre salary of £80 a year, especially as one of my junior assistants earned more than I did because he was a male. At this time there was considerable prejudice against college graduates, for the university course had only been in existence for about four or five years and was not backed up by practical experience. However, I did know quite a lot about books and as I read a great deal, I was able to fill the gaps in my knowledge of fiction so as to be able to help my borrowers. I read samples of the popular authors of 'westerns', 'romances' and detective stories whose work I did not know, and was soon able to be of more assistance to my borrowers even if I did not always share their choice. Apart from books, it was the borrowers I was interested in and these were friendly once they were used to my London accent. Soon I knew the 'regulars' that haunt all libraries. "A romance, luv," a woman would say trustingly, producing her book from the basket in which she was carrying the strong-smelling fish for her 'hubby's' dinner. "You know what I like," someone would say – and I did know, more or less.

I don't think I was much loved by the junior assistants who worked with me, for I believed that the books on the shelves must be in order and I kept the unfortunate young people searching for the endless 'queries' (which they had made themselves when discharging the books at busy periods). I knew that all must be in apple pie order when the Chief Librarian came on his visit of inspection.

The Chief, an eminent librarian, who had a talent for organisation, had begun his career at the age of thirteen in 1884 and had been appointed to Bolton in 1904, a daunting thought as I was only born that year! He valued knowledge and insisted on all assistants having Matriculation as their minimum educational qualification. Perhaps this was the reason he had given me a post, for I was the first of his assistants to have a university education.

But to most of us, the Chief was an awe-inspiring figure who could make or break us. His office was across the square, so the Deputy Librarian was able to warn us when he set out to honour us with his daily visit. At the whisper, "The Chief is on his way!" we would hastily busy ourselves so as to give an air of great efficiency. Offending items would be swept out of sight and we would line up as if for a military inspection, for he was something of a martinet. Surprisingly, he was quite a small man, but made up for this with waxed moustaches, and he had the distinction of being the only man in Bolton to wear a top-hat daily. It *seemed* that his most scathing criticisms were directed at the female and the more sensitive assistants, and I cannot imagine any of his staff being on informal terms with him, but perhaps I do him an injustice. The modern custom of library staff addressing their Chiefs by their Christian names would have been *unthinkable* with this Chief of old days.

I was two years in Bolton, a lonely experience, except when a colleague shared my lodging with me for a time. She too suffered, for she had been educated at Cheltenham College for Ladies and her accent showed this. She escaped to a more congenial post as soon as she could. We became lifelong friends and our companionship was a happy one for we could discuss books and work. Sometimes she would come in boiling with exasperation after a 'state visit' of the Chief to her branch.

At first, my only experience of work with children was an occasional half hour in a dark corner where children came to borrow books. There was no access to the shelves – an indicator showed what books were in and could be asked for. This meant I had no contact with my borrowers. On one occasion I was reminded of their home background for I was handed a book in which a chipped potato had been used as a bookmark!

It is relevant to consider the state of library service to children in the early 1920s. It was scarcely encouraging for in the seventy-five years or so since the inauguration of the Public Library Service in 1850, little notice had been taken of children's book needs. What progress there had been was usually due to the enthusiasm of an individual rather than a definite policy of service. Reading Rooms for children had been set up in the 1860s at Manchester, Birkenhead and Birmingham, but these were largely in response to social need. By 1898, however, 110 libraries made some provision for books for children. It must be remembered that until 1919, the library rate could not be more than a penny in the pound so that, with the priorities of the time, there was a reluctance to - and every antagonism against - spending money on books for children. The appearance and furniture of children's rooms reflected this attitude. As late as 1912, Leeds children's department was up a steep flight of stairs, badly lit and furnished with high tables and backless forms. I had found similar unsuitable provision in public libraries in Fulham in 1924. In the 1920s there were still many libraries which denied children access to the shelves, as in the Central Library in Bolton.

Library books, too, often *looked* forbidding because of their gloomy binding. Our own Chief at Bolton had recommended at one time that children's books should be bought *already bound* in half hog-skin so that they would never need re-binding. The depressing effects of this economy measure was still to be seen when I was there.

Children's librarians were non-existent.   In 1907, Cardiff had appointed a Lady Superintendent to be in charge of the Reading Room; but there was a general feeling that 'ladies' would not be able to keep the older boys (and girls?) in order.   Children were often not allowed to join the library under the age of seven, or even ten, on the ground that they wouldn't behave themselves, and anyway there weren't enough books of a suitable kind for them.   This at a period when authors and artists, such as Walter Crane, were producing their picture books.

But the cause of book provision for children had strong support from such far-seeing and outstanding librarians as L.S. Jast, J. Ballinger, J.D. Stewart and Berwick Sayers.   The latter had instituted a model children's room at Croydon.   It was light, suitably furnished, had open access and a children's librarian, Ethel Hayler, who ran activities such as story-telling.   Leeds was taken in hand by another devoted librarian, Mrs M. Hummerston, who made it a live department from 1912 to 1947, after which time children's libraries were sadly not considered necessary.

By 1917, the Library Association could acknowledge that library work with children ought to be the basis of all library work, and even admitted the desirability of appointing trained librarians to work with children.

This then was the climate in which I had the temerity to believe that some day I would have a children's library of my own in which the children would be free to enjoy books in attractive surroundings.   Bolton gave me the first opportunity to realise a tiny modicum of my wish, for I was put in charge of the children's room in a new branch.   There was open access, the room was light and I could really meet the children. Most of my time, of course, was taken up by routine duties such as issuing and discharging books, compiling a catalogue and preparing books for circulation.   But I did occasionally have time to walk amongst the children and help them to choose their books.   I even planned to hold a Storytime and designed a poster to advertise this innovation. Unfortunately, this work of art was visible when the Chief came on one of his visits.   His reaction was to tell me to remove it and then to inform me that "If I had time to tell stories, some more useful work could be found for me".   However I did manage a story or two and the children enjoyed them.   The older boys and girls in their teens, known as 'little piecers' because they joined broken threads in the cotton mills, were sometimes a problem.   I was small and fair game for them, nothing malicious really.   One of their ploys was to follow behind me chanting

"See 'er marching down the street
Wiv 'er Rooshians on 'er feet..."

Hours were long and the libraries were open until 9.00pm, and if I was sent to be in charge of a branch in the evening this meant a late night. Coming home on dark rainy nights by tram or foot was not enjoyable, but streets were safe in those days, and I was never molested in any way. Saturday half-days were few and far between, but this was an occupational hazard for which I was prepared, and anyway I had nowhere to go, except for walks.

In my lodgings, my landlady sat each evening in her rocking chair, doing 'nuffing at all', and when she considered it was time for bed (for me as well as her), she took down her hair and plaited it. Sometimes when my colleague was sharing with me, we would stay up, greatly daring, after she had gone to bed. Occasionally a neighbour, a cheery little woman, would come in to visit, bringing her son Freddie of eleven or so. He was liable, at the least encouragement, to recite such dramatic gems as *The Charge of the Light Brigade*, while his fond mother beamed with pride. On other occasions, Mrs Shaw would be wrapped in gloom all day to celebrate the anniversary of her husband's death, or some other 'happy' event. But we got on well together, for I appreciated her care for me and her essential goodness and uprightness.

So two years passed. I was gaining experience and maturity, a better foundation for a future post. Once a year I escaped for ten days or a fortnight. This was usually the 'Wakes' week when everything – shops, mills, life – seemed to stand still and most of the population set out for the seaside. The station was crowded, there were queues outside, everyone was happy and excited and good humoured and ready for a spending spree. It was rumoured that most people spent everything they had, leaving just enough at home to tide them over for the next day. I escaped too with a joyful heart, to see my mother and sister, or my father, with whom I always kept in touch.

One day I saw an advertisement which was to alter my life. It was for a 'Part-time, Temporary Assistant' to organise a library service for children in a place called Hendon in the North-West of London. This was my chance at last!

I hurried to the Chief to ask for a testimonial to back up my application for this unusual post. He was horrified. What, give up a permanent post for one which was temporary only? I was mad. However, I insisted, my knees knocking together with fright at my temerity. "But this Authority wants someone with initiative and discretion," he said. "I am not aware that you have either." This devastating comment filled me with courage. "What chance have I had to show initiative here?" So I sent off my application and received a reply telling me what the successful applicant would be expected to do. Once again this cautious Authority reminded me that the appointment was temporary only and would not necessarily guarantee a post when the new library was built. But I still considered it a good risk. To establish a library system could not be part-time for long and it was surely up to me to prove myself a suitable and capable assistant for the post of Children's Librarian when the library materialised. Even to think of the possibility filled me with hope and excitement. So I gathered my testimonials together and sent them off. Looking at them I was surprised to discover that the director of the School of Librarianship stated that I had an "exceedingly wide knowledge of children's books" and that I had "indefatigable energy"! Even my former headmistress had some quite pleasant things to say of me (with no mention of my abysmal record in mathematics).

After the usual delay, which seems interminable to an applicant, I was called for an interview and travelled to London, and so to Hendon. It was a sunny day in August and as I walked up the hill from the Underground station – the line had only reached Hendon three years previously – there seemed a freshness and cleanliness about it that was a welcome change after the harsher face of a Northern provincial town. The Town Hall, at that time a very modest building, was pleasant and homely, in spite of the vast statue of Sir Stamford Raffles in the entrance. The half-dozen other applicants for the post seemed to have an alarming self-confidence and they were certainly much larger than I was! The committee was kindly and I at once noticed the chairman particularly, a woman of dignity and authority. (I discovered later that the imaginative idea of establishing a library system beginning with children was hers.) I soon sensed that she was the guiding spirit of the committee and that the applicant who pleased her would have a good chance of being appointed. I answered the sometimes irrelevant questions of the councillors as well as I could (one asked me if I could play the organ). I could not pretend that I was vastly experienced but I did feel that I had considerable knowledge of children's books – and of children – and I could claim in all sincerity that my greatest wish and ambition was to work with children. I realised with growing confidence that the chairman, Mrs Bannister, was interested. I suspect it helped that I had a university education and had read widely, for she was an ex-His Majesty's Inspector and had been principal of a Teacher Training College.

I awaited in a fever of hope in the ante-room – and was recalled and offered the post. I accepted with alacrity, trying to appear calm and worthy of the trust that was to be put in me. The salary was a little over £100 a year for the part-time post not much to live on, but better than my *very* full-time post at Bolton which only brought my £80.

I returned to Bolton with confidence and hope. I was only twenty-two and the world was before me. My first task was to tell the Chief of my good fortune. He received me with disapproval at my folly but informed me graciously that, as I would *of course* have no idea of how to begin the task of organising a library system, I was welcome to appeal to his staff for advice. I never did.

Eileen, September 1982, with 'Jacko', the glove puppet

Eileen, aged 2, Robin Hood's Bay

The Colwell Family, Bradford-on-Avon
(back): Father; Eric
(middle): Dell; Eileen; Mother
(front): Vera

Above: Hendon Junior Library Helpers
Below: Storytime, with a rapt audience

Eileen, the Librarian

Above: Telling the tale at the Boys and Girls House, Toronto

Below: Study time: homework in the Library

Hendon Junior Library Helpers in charge

Above: at a seminar for 50 librarians,
Hakone, within sight of Mount Fuji

Below: Eileen Colwell, Doctor of Literature

PART THREE
BUILDING A LIBRARY

CHAPTER EIGHT

So in September 1926 I travelled to Hendon once more to take up my duties. Lodgings had been found for me in a quiet street within walking distance of the Town Hall where I was to have my headquarters. Paying for my lodgings took up most of my salary, but I would manage for my wants were few, as long as I had access to books and work that interested me. The local Methodist church provided me with a chance to make friends, especially as one of the councillors was a Methodist and took a kindly interest in my welfare.

Hendon at this time was almost rural, with open spaces and many trees and its ancient church set on a hill. There were almshouses and a forge still in working order. The village pond, which had been a watersplash, was now confined within railings but it reminded one of days not so long ago. The chief claim to fame of the area was the aerodrome. Grahame-White had bought pasture land in 1910 and converted it into the London Aerodrome and this became one of the best known and completely organised airfields in the world. The first UK Aerial Post was flown from Hendon to Windsor, and Hendon's flying displays became an event which brought thousands to view them, many making a day of it in the Sunnyhill Fields which overlooked the aerodrome. By 1926 the aerodrome had passed out of private ownership to become an RAF station. It was this association with the development of aviation and the coming of the Underground railway that had changed Hendon from a village to a town.

On arrival at the Town Hall, I was welcomed by a friendly official who showed me the room where I was to work, a large room with a generous fireplace, which had been used as a members' common room. I sat down to survey the situation. All I had was the use of a room, a limited amount of money – the Library Rate had been levied for a year without any expenditure. I had no shelves for the books I was to buy; I had no stationery, no typewriter, no assistants and not a single book. I had to create a library service for children within three months for it was billed to open in January 1927.

But I had one valuable asset: Councillor Mrs Bannister, and no one could have wished for more. Mrs Bannister had no knowledge of librarianship, but she had been an administrator and she knew all the people who mattered in the district. At once, she took me round the seven schools that had been chosen as distributing centres and introduced me personally to the head teachers, thus ensuring their co-operation. These centres were to open for one or two evenings a week with the aid of voluntary helpers found by Mrs Bannister from her friends and contacts. So I had an unpaid but highly cultured 'staff' which included a journalist, housewife and a retired teacher with means and time to spare, and some young people who were students, two of whom became librarians.

The situation in Hendon was unusual as regards libraries. Hendon was still an Urban District and only achieved the status of a Borough three years after I arrived. A plan for a library system had been mooted in 1914, but the War had caused it to be shelved. In 1919 the Public Libraries Acts had been adopted and the first Libraries Committee convened but post-war crises had stopped the implementation of the Act until 1925, when the Library Rate of one penny was imposed and the UK Carnegie Trust promised £7,000 towards a library building. Due, I suspect, to the foresight of Mrs Bannister, it was proposed that a library system should be inaugurated *beginning with the children*, a most unusual course, but a wise one, for it would create a nucleus of borrowers who would be ready to support the library when it came and would also arouse the interest of the public in a scheme which could be seen to succeed. Mrs Bannister, as an educator, believed wholeheartedly in the value of establishing the reading habit amongst children.

This was the background of my appointment and surely it was a unique opportunity and a challenge. From the beginning, I had the Libraries Committee behind me, a friendly committee. Once they realised that they had an assistant who was an enthusiast and a book lover, one who did not work by the clock but rather ignored it, I was assured of help, for they were anxious for the success of their unconventional approach to the creation of the long-awaited library system.

My first task was to put in hand the shelving of my room and the design and printing of stationery ready for the books I was to buy. Middlesex County had agreed to lend 800 books – to be chosen by me – and to exchange them when necessary. The rest of the stock I was to select and buy, and for this purpose Mrs Bannister again came to my help by introducing me to Eleanor Graham, critic, author and later editor of Puffin Books, who at that time was in charge of the Children's Book Department at Bumpus Books. She gave me expert advice on my choice from her personal knowledge, for she was engaged at that time in 'reading round the shelves' so that she would know every book in her stock. We exchanged book-knowledge happily and she became a friend as well as a mentor. I was also introduced to the Foyle family of book-shop fame (a contact with which I was far less happy).

From almost the first moment it was obvious that this would never be a part-time post, for there was far too much to do in the buying and preparation of books for circulation. A friend of Mrs Bannister's from one of the best-known old families in Hendon came cheerfully to help me to label books and write book-cards; in fact anything menial that I required. I have never bought books from catalogues and have always insisted on *seeing* a book before purchase, so that I was building up knowledge of children's books all the time, a process which has never ceased all my life. All these activities had occupied my *whole* time happily from the beginning and, in January 1927, I was appointed *officially* full-time and my salary increased to £180 annually, which I considered riches!

So in January 1927 the Hendon library system began, and I visited my first centre and issued the first book ever issued from Hendon Libraries. Appropriately enough it was *Little Women*. I remember the child who borrowed it too. Like the other children, she had rushed home to have her form signed and was the first to arrive back again. Her name was Annie and she lived in Lovejoy Cottages, and her round rosy face beamed at me from her 'pixie hood' as she brought the new book with its spotless dustjacket to be stamped. She was making history unwittingly, the first child borrower of the thousands that were to come. There had been no formal opening with speeches from officials, but the occasion was a success. At the end of the hour, twenty-five children in a rural part of Hendon had made their first visit to a library and chosen their own books.

My centres were in different parts of Hendon, three were in industrial areas, two in residential districts, this one almost in the country, and the seventh in a school attended chiefly by children from a council orphanage. 'Library Evening' was an 'occasion' to these children especially, for they were not usually allowed to come out after school hours and there were few treats in their ordered lives.

Before the year was out there were several new centres, one in a welfare service hut, the other in a church. Here, the absent-minded vicar would come and look at me in amazement, having quite forgotten that the hall was being used as a library. Another centre was at a co-educational school at Golders Green, where the children wandered into the library only if they *felt* like reading on that particular day, and the headmaster was located mending the roof.

By the end of the first year over 25,000 books had been issued and by the end of the second (1928), 65,000. The scheme was a success. I had been able to arrange some extra activities; a Book Week for instance, during which I visited schools and told stories and talked about books, or brought in someone interesting to talk to the children. I had little time or facilities to arrange such activities regularly. That must come when the main library was built. The foundation stone was to be laid by Mrs Bannister in 1928. I looked forward to having a library in which I could find books to answer the requests I received so frequently from my children, requests I had no means of satisfying without a central stock of books behind me.

There was still no Chief Librarian to organise the whole adult system but one was to be appointed in early 1929. I had the fun of taking a substantial part in choosing my own Chief, for the list of applicants was brought to me and I was asked to look through it and indicate those I thought the best qualified and whose reputation I knew. I picked a couple, one of them being the chief of the library where I had worked for three months when I was a student. (Incidentally, he could never remember the temporary student he had sent to a branch.) This was the one who was appointed – and who was my Chief from 1927 for over twenty years. I had chosen well, both for the council and myself, for Mr Walker was helpful and kind to me always, giving me opportunities to carry out new ideas and backing me up in all my activities.

For three months I had a Chief Librarian all to myself and a strenuous time it was! I acted as secretary, typing out book order lists and cutting stencils (very badly), checking the books as they arrived. I grew to dread the endless boxes of cards which I must check as Mr Walker read out lists. I dreamed cards… In my few spare moments I made a start on my own booklists for the children's department I was to run, for I had now been appointed as Hendon's first Children's Librarian at a salary of £240 per annum. At the same time I must keep the system I had created running smoothly, for I could not disappoint my own borrowers. I had fourteen centres now and about 5,000 borrowers. My job had become full-time with a vengeance - morning, afternoon and evening. But I enjoyed it all, and it never occurred to me that perhaps I deserved overtime pay.

In April, several members of staff were appointed, including a typist. I was able to hand over that part of my duties with a sigh of relief and concentrate on the selection of my own two thousand books and the plans for my future library. To have hundreds of pounds to spend on books was a delightful and satisfying experience, a pleasure that never palled in my forty years service with children and books.

The library building had been started in April 1928 on a site between the Town Hall and the Fire Station, a prudent arrangement providing for its financial and physical safety. When the workmen had gone home, I often wandered round the building to gloat over the space where I knew my department was to be. The exterior of the building was most imposing, flanked by lofty Corinthian columns. There was a feeling of spaciousness about it, although the interior had functional faults known only to the staff : no staff-room; the only access to the work room through the reference library, a department supposed to be devoted to study in a reverential silence. Whenever the staff tiptoed through this room every head turned. When he came, Mr Walker had done what he could to correct obvious errors, but the building was too far advanced for him to do all that he knew was necessary. It was to be years before some of the basic faults could be rectified.

The library was to be opened in December 1929. The public little knew how unlikely this seemed the day before. The whole staff worked until late at night, shelving the last books, arranging displays, while the cleaning staff polished 'with all their might and main'. At eight o'clock that evening the Chief decreed that we must have a break and something to eat. For the first and last time in the history of the library, the staff sat down to eat at a trestle table between the shelves – what did we eat? The proverbial food of the Englishman in the 20th century, of course: fish and chips, washed down with tea. For us it was a festival day, for we could now see the result of our hard work. At midnight the last touch had been given and I set out to walk to my lodgings, accompanied by the Chief in case I met with any mishap on the lonely roads.

The next morning the cleaning staff literally swept out of the back door as the front door was ceremoniously opened by the Earl of Elgin, Chairman of the United Kingdom Carnegie Trust. His speech was broadcast on 2LO, a mark of the importance of the occasion, for Hendon Library was the largest public library building to be erected in England since the First World War. It had cost £37,000, a large sum then although it would be considered derisory now. Hendon's library became a showpiece and was a Mecca for overseas visitors. The fittings were considered the last word in efficiency – the stockrooms with their metal shelving; the glass floors to give extra light; a book lift to the upper floors; bookcases floodlit from above, the lower shelves tilted backwards so that no stooping was necessary to read the book titles.

The opening of the Library was a triumph for the Council's policy, especially for Mrs Bannister who, as chairman of the Libraries Committee from 1919 to 1930, had done so much to bring it about. The policy of creating a library service beginning with children had been shown to be a success and had paved the way for the more extensive service which had always been envisaged for adults. Few members of the committee, however, can have foreseen how wide-spread the service would become, with its branch libraries, travelling libraries, universal school library system and museum.

After the official opening, the library was opened for the public to inspect, for it was *their* library and they had a right to see what they had provided for the community. Members of the staff stood proudly in their departments, ready to point out its glories. Hordes of children swept through the children's room, exclaiming and looking for their favourite books. "We'll be back on Monday, Miss," they said and I hoped with all my heart that they would.

When they had all gone, I looked round my room with pride and joy. It was a large and attractive room – Mrs Bannister had laid claim for it because it was the sunniest room in the building. There were over two thousand books on the shelves, all new and in their dust jackets. There were flowers on the sills of the lofty windows, colourful posters and displays. The tables, both oblong and round, were of solid oak – they would be considered too formal today, but they gave good service and withstood the depredations of children for half a century. It was a welcoming room.

When the children had gone, chattering and excited, I lingered for a moment alone, savouring my moment of achievement. My dream of so long had almost come true. Here was my library and here were the books. All that was needed now was the children and it was evident there would be no lack of them. With their coming, the library and the books would come to life. This library belonged to children – it was their dream and mine now. Together we would make it a happy place.

CHAPTER NINE

The first day of opening came and with it crowds of children, hurrying in with their application forms already signed, eager to secure the books they had seen on the first night. I wasted no time but at once enlisted some of them as 'Helpers', *not* as a cheap source of aid to relieve myself of routine duties but because I believed in giving children responsibility. I believed, too, that the children would have more respect for the library and its contents if they were involved in its running. The post of Library Helper became much sought after, even though would-be helpers had to pass a test in issue methods and the layout of the library and the use of the catalogue. A girl of nine speaking at one of our Parents Evenings said, "Sometimes you are sad and lonely if you can't be a helper right away but if you are patient, you get to be one at last."

The tradition of Junior Library Helpers lasted for the forty years I was in charge. Hundreds of children enjoyed the experience of helping in their own library as a *privilege*, for there were no rewards of any kind. Only once do I remember a boy asking how much he would be paid. "But it's *fun!*" exclaimed his companions. The helpers were often more careful and conscientious than paid assistants – they were certainly more adamant on the payment of fines and in matters of behaviour. At one time when we had a Library Committee of children, the chairman addressed the members thus: "Ladies and gentlemen, I would like to call your attention to the fact that *some* children scribble in library books" (fixing a small frightened boy with his eyes). "Something will happen to such boys! No boy or girl who does not pay his fines should be allowed in again – we will know who we mean." (Another boy visibly wilted in his chair.) For we librarians the helpers were a source of opinions about the books they had read, critics of what went on in the library – and friends.

From the first I hoped to encourage a feeling of freedom and happiness in the library. I did not believe in imposing silence (usually expected at that time), for silence is unnatural to any child. Conversation was in order as long as it did not disturb the children who wanted to read – although children reading can be completely oblivious of everything that goes on around them. I *expected* good behaviour and

I had only to speak to a child who was being anti-social to achieve it. Most of my 'children' were taller than I was, but I scarcely ever knew them contest my authority, probably because they knew I only used it when necessary. Children appreciate knowing how far they can go with impunity.

The first year was extremely busy. By the end of it, I and my one assistant (who had been a former voluntary assistant in my centres), issued 65,000 books and I had to increase my stock substantially. I still had two of my original centres to administer – these were being retained as a forerunner of the branch libraries which must eventually be provided in those areas (Golders Green and Mill Hill). The rest of my stock had been handed over to the Education Authority to form the nucleus of a school library system. The ultimate aim was to establish an adequate library at every school in the borough, which would provide general reading and a liberal supply of books on school subjects. This aim was achieved as the population grew and new schools were opened.

I was extremely fortunate in having a Chief Librarian who believed that the foundation of all library work was laid in the children's department, an attitude which was extremely rare at that time. He did not consider either, as did so many librarians, that if economy was necessary, the children's department should be the first to suffer.

As soon as the library was in running order, I inaugurated activities for the pleasure of the children and as a means of encouraging interest in books. First my abiding interest, storytelling. Weekly Story Hours were begun for children of any age and from 1933 these were augmented, to the children's delight, by a Story Festival in the Christmas holidays. In practise, the children's ages varied from 7 to 11, plus a sprinkling of younger brothers and sisters who could not be left out. Attendance was entirely voluntary, so it was our responsibility to win a child's interest. We realised that low attendance was usually due to an unwise choice of story or our own inadequacies as storytellers. My assistants were expected to take a turn and I suspect that to tell stories was a real trial to many of these beginners. Some felt too nervous to try; a few resented this call on their time, for the preparation of the stories often had to be done in their leisure hours. But many enjoyed the experience and the knowledge it gave them of literature and became expert storytellers. I was surprised and touched in the years that followed to hear adults say, "Do you remember that story you used to tell about...? I have never forgotten it and I tell it to my own children now." Such is the abiding magic of a good story, although storytellers seldom have the rewards of knowing the influence of a story on a child's imagination and heart.

Another source of interest to the children was the series of talks and lectures arranged for them, often illustrated by lantern slides, the 'television' of the day. These were during school hours and attended by a 'captive' audience who probably regarded them as a welcome escape from school lessons! The subject could be anything from a recital in costume, an illustrated talk on natural history, or a travel talk. The lecturers included indigent authors, travellers, naturalists, and even an expert on armour who appeared (most uncomfortably) in a complete suit of armour which clanked as he walked in. I remember Geoffrey Trease as a young author; Captain Knight, who brought a real live eagle with him, much to the disgust of the caretaker for it was not 'house trained'; Noel Streatfeild, author of *Ballet Shoes,* who thrilled the older girls with her sophisticated and glamorous appearance. A real 'seadog', Captain Course, recounted his adventures. George Cansdale of London Zoo came with two rats, a chinchilla and a boa-constrictor several feet long, as company. One of the children said solicitously, "I do hope the snake who is changing his skin won't find some of the bits missing!" Some were invited to hold the animals, but first Mr Cansdale said, "Don't be afraid of holding the snake – it's quite pleasant!" He draped the boa-constrictor round my neck as he spoke. "See, your Children's Librarian doesn't mind at all." (She was terrified.)

In 1930, the year the library opened, I planned a library magazine for children called the *Magic Casement,* which continued until 1936. It was issued quarterly and was free to children. It contained a brief introductory article about an author or some subject of interest such as camping, the Coronation, the circus. An annotated booklist arranged under interesting headings followed, and notes on book news.

Re-reading these productions of my youthful enthusiasm after a long interval, I think that perhaps they did warrant the comment in a contemporary library periodical, as being 'free from pedantry...neither pompous nor gushing...' (*Lib. Assist.,* August 1930 and December 1931).

Of course we had clubs for the children - always popular, but transient when some new interest took their place. So we ran a Library Club, a Stamp Club, a Music Club. A Zoo Club brought various pets to the library whose presence was not always appreciated – a slow worm, a tortoise, a stick insect (which was donated to the library and left to our reluctant care). The assistant caretaker, a gardening enthusiast, made history by giving a talk about "them there bees" in his garden. I applied one criterion, however, to every club: that it must involve and encourage the use of books; if it did not, the library was no place for it. We had a good stock of books and could always back up any legitimate activity.

Book Weeks soon became an annual feature. I had held one of my own in 1928, long before such activities became a national gesture by the National Book League. In 1932 we were able to hold one on a much larger scale, with visiting authors, school visits, displays and exhibitions, book quizzes and competitions. Such affairs need careful organisation so that the speakers are assured of the right kind of audience for their particular approach. I am reminded of an occasion when I visited a London library to hear the actor Robert Speaight speak to children. Instead of the older boys and girls he expected, due to a lack of organisation there was an audience of children aged six to seven. The poor man was quite unable to adapt himself and began to speak of the problems of *Hamlet*. It did occur to him after a time that perhaps children of this age might not be familiar with the play, or even know anything about Shakespeare. So he said, tentatively, "Has anyone here read *Hamlet*?" "Yes," said a little girl of six, shooting up her hand eagerly; what she thought she was saying 'Yes' to, no one knew. The lecturer continued doggedly with his planned talk, but every now and then he appealed for confirmation to "my friend in the front row". Each time, she nodded with a pleased smile at the attention she was receiving.

One thing I was always careful about was to meet the speakers on their arrival at the station, to treat them with courtesy and plan for their comfort, and to arrange for them to be paid on the spot! Sadly, lecturers were often treated with less than courtesy and there were many 'horror' tales told on the lecturers' circuit. Later, when I was a lecturer myself, I discovered how casual people can be: no one to open the hall where I was to speak; being rushed straight on to the platform after a long journey with no opportunity to 'tidy up'; the lecture timed so that it was impossible for me to have a meal; and numerous other incivilities due to thoughtlessness.

Too often, parents and teachers are unaware of the extent of the work that goes on in a children's department and the standard of service provided in book selection. So for many years Hendon held a Parents' Evening. A councillor opened the proceedings (I often wrote his speech at his request so that he said the right things). This was followed by a play acted by the children, and usually written by me to suit the inadequacies of the stage and the limited talent available. So we did scenes from *Little Women*; a *Book Dream*, so that a number of book characters could he introduced; *Emil and the Detectives*, in which the hilarious pursuit of the Man in the Bowler Hat involved the whole audience. We even did a Chinese play in full costume (adapted from Lewis' *Ho-Ming*). The costumes were available because of the missionary plays my mother put on in our manse days. To produce a play successfully with fourteen or fifteen excited children, no dressing room, makeshift curtains and lights, and on a platform about 18" high, was quite an achievement, a co-operative effort of children, librarians and caretaker and helpful parents. Sometimes the children wrote descriptions of the library activities and delivered them on the night. These could be disconcerting but were presented sincerely, proving the speakers' involvement with their library. Quite often a local school contributed music or verse-speaking. The evening closed with story from me.

Every occasion of this kind was accompanied by an exhibition of books to interest children and parents alike. Indeed, the introduction of books should be the main reason and inspiration of all library activities. My personal opinion was, and still is, that this is what a library is for.

The relationship between the library and the schools was always cordial in Hendon, perhaps because we had worked together before there was a library. Now that a school library system was being built up there were many ways in which we could co-operate. Before long, classes were visiting the library not only to learn about its services (which would be of value to us) but also to find material for individual projects (which benefited the teachers). In 1933 there were twenty-nine school libraries, by 1934 thirty-one, for the borough was developing all the time. So one of my earliest ideas to help teachers was in establishing a picture collection. The material was obtained from old numbers of periodicals like the *Illustrated London News*, *National Geographic* and other suitable magazines. I was allowed to spend money on the collection too, so bought sets of British Birds, Costume, Authors, indeed any source I could discover. Each illustration had to be mounted on standard sized paper, classified and filed. Eventually this collection numbered thousands and a special fitment had to be provided to accommodate it. It was used not only by teachers and children, but by commercial artists (one contributed a cartoon which said 'If you can't find it at the British Museum, try Colwell's place') and even the BBC. The labour involved was considerable but here again the older boys and girls helped to mount, label and even to classify. I had also begun to assemble a collection of books and handicrafts of the kind taught in schools and this functioned for many years.   Any books, pictures, sets of plays were issued to teachers for an extended period to suit their needs and there was no question of fines for overdue items.

All these activities were signs of a busy and thriving library and developed naturally from any contact with children and books.

CHAPTER TEN

In 1931 I was in a position to buy a house so that I could give my mother and my younger sister a home. My mother had managed to support herself and my sister ever since the separation – one can only surmise what this had cost her in effort and determination. During the ten years before I was able to buy a house for us all at Hendon, my mother had a variety of positions. One was as custodian of an old manor house with a café, by the river in Knaresborough, Yorkshire. Another was as housekeeper and cook in a Christian Endeavour Holiday Home near Snowdon, North Wales. She gained most satisfaction from the time she spent running her own business, a village shop in Kirkby-in-Furness on the Lakeland border. This gave her independence and scope for initiative. She was now sixty-three and very weary. Vera enjoyed the contact with people and the surrounding countryside and had undertaken such work as she could find without training of any kind.

We settled down happily together. It was very pleasant for me to have my family with me, and my mother, after her many years of 'ministerial' furniture and the three-yearly move, took quiet pleasure in choosing her own surroundings and feeling that she had security. Her great delight was the small greenhouse I managed to give her, for she loved growing things, as did Vera.

We were fortunate in that our house abutted on a sliver of woodland beyond which was the railway line in a deep cutting. This land, I discovered, I could rent from the railway so that we looked out on trees and could grow woodland flowers. There were hedgehogs there, regarded with much curiosity by our dog. Our home was open to young women who were away from home or needed friendship. These we came across in our Methodist church. We enjoyed their company and became friends.

In the years immediately before war broke out, I enjoyed my first two trips abroad. In 1934, I went to Holland, the first of many visits to that country. I enjoyed Holland very much, with its canals, dykes and flowers. My Dutch hosts were kind and the son of the house escorted me to see the tourist attractions. In return, Mr Wagnaar, an older man, came to stay with my family. He was a very tall man and arrived with a sheaf of gladioli as tall as himself. He also had a large capacity for substantial food – like most Dutchmen – and taxed our household larder considerably. However, he was kind, and we managed to converse in short sentences helped out with gestures and drawings.

My second trip was a most interesting one. It took place in 1938, at the time when Hitler was invading Sudetenland. A German friend was to accompany me to a Wagner festival at Lippe Detmold. I first stayed with her parents, her father was a Lutheran pastor in Bulefuld. They were a kind, homely couple, much perplexed at what was happening in Germany. They took me, rather oddly, to see a home for epileptics, the largest in Europe.

Martha and I went to the festival where we stayed in a hostel for visitors and fifty Hitler Jugend. They paraded each morning to salute Hitler's swastika. One night, the leader of the Hitler Jugend asked Martha, "Does the little Englander understand what we are saying?" I did! It was 'When we march down the streets of Paris...When we march down the streets of London...'

Conditions at the hostel were primitive – we women paraded in a large wash room where ample German women played naked under an icy hose with much merriment. One morning we rose at 6am and walked to pay our respects to an enormous statue – Hermann, a traditional hero who freed the people from the Romans long, long ago. On the way back, the company sang a hymn to Hitler. Everyone, especially the women, said how kind Hitler was and how he worked for the people and was one of them.

At the opera – which was magnificent, sung by international soloists – the performance was always prefaced by a speech an hour long by a Gauleiter and was followed by fervid shouts of *"Heil Hitler!"*, I always said "God save the King". Fortunately, I was not arrested. On the last night, *The Meistersingers,* with its central figure Hans Sachs and the beautiful 'Prize Song' tenor solo, was performed, lasting six hours.

With the music still ringing in my ears, my visit ended. An experience not to be forgotten in the light of what followed so soon after when 'the lights went out' in Europe.

Then the War came. I remember the first day vividly! As we were about household tasks on that sunny Sunday morning, we heard the banshee wail of the first siren, a sound which can still send a cold shiver down my spine.

In those first days of the War it was anticipated that the Germans would make a lightening raid on London before our forces were ready to defend us.

Air raid warnings were frequent, mostly false, but every time I had to take the children who were about to an air raid shelter. There, we told them stories or entertained them somehow. As it happened, that first year was the 'Phoney War'. Trenches were dug in parks, buildings were sandbagged. My mother had a weak heart, so she and my sister went to the home of a school-friend in the North of England, where an attack was unlikely. I could not move myself, of course. In fact, as libraries were staffed largely by women (for the men who were eligible were called up), I was busier than ever and took on extra responsibilities.

Libraries were well used during the War, perhaps because reading provided a welcome temporary escape from the terrors and hardships and relieved the tedium of the long hours of the 'blackout'. In fact, two branch libraries were erected, one at Golders Green and the other at Mill Hill.

I had often to be in charge of the Central Library while the Chief Librarian was on duty – like many older men – watching for the approach of enemy 'planes. Public talks and lectures had to be in abeyance because of the danger of air raids and the library was a centre for War efforts. In fact, it was this that brought me an unusual encounter, for the Queen (now the Queen Mother) came to Hendon Library in connection with the borough's Four Fighter Fund. On her way out she asked to see the Children's Library. I was in the counter, standing on a box in order to see the Queen approaching, when she was ushered in without warning. She was dressed in her favourite violet colour (with an elegant hat, of course) and I saw that she was not much taller then me. At once, she asked me if I could recommend some good authors for her daughters (the Princesses). I quite forgot that she was the Queen and we talked about children and books quite at ease for several minutes. This was the secret of her popularity with the people, which has lasted to the present day. She has a warmth of character, and ease with ordinary people which our present Queen has never quite achieved, well intentioned as she is.

Civilians were trained to deal with air raids. I presented myself therefore. There were difficulties – there were no steel hats small enough for me. I had to take one which spun round my small head. We had to crawl through a smoke chamber with a hose, during which ordeal my too-large Wellington boots fell off and the man who crawled after me had to push them – and me – in front of him. At stated times I was on duty, equipped with whistle and spinning steel hat, gas mask at the ready, to watch for enemy 'planes! I spent lonely hours on duty – not that I should have been of much use, I imagine.

After some months, my mother and Vera returned home from their exile. It had been an unhappy and upsetting time. It was joy to be together again, especially at Christmas, when we were joined by a neighbour, Una Morris, who had had to take up War work. New neighbours had come, a family of German Jewish refugees, a sign of the terrible treatment of Jews by Hitler, the appalling cruelty of which we did not know at the time.

Then the bombing raids began. I had an Anderson shelter dug out in the extension of our garden. It was several feet deep, and of cement and was chill and grey and confined. We had a bed, a lamp and a couple of chairs put there. When the siren wailed, we all trooped out carrying blankets, descended into its chilly depths, listened for the planes and bombs and waited for the 'German Invasion' from next door. The Jewish family took it for granted that they might share our shelter. We were three, and now we were expected to find room for the old parent, the daughter-in-law and two boys. After a few nights of near suffocation I had to insist that we could only accommodate three persons, the younger woman and the older boy must remain indoors, except in emergencies. The next night, a bomb fell with its customary *whoosh!* At once, Frau M and her son came screaming down the garden with the boy spurting ahead. Eight people in a shelter for four – this was WAR! A quotation from the diary I kept at the time will suffice to show what life was like.

> We hurried back through the pitch darkness. As we opened the door, we heard a plane flying very low. Then came a sound like an express train. We dived under the stairs. The whole house shook under us and then there was dead silence which seemed even more terrifying. Only then did the warning sound and quite soon after that the All Clear. We found the front door was blown open. In the kitchen the floor was covered with treacle. A jar had been blown off a shelf and burst open. The next morning we heard to our horror that the flying torpedo had fallen in West Hendon and, as no warning had been given, over a hundred people had been killed and one thousand made homeless.

Lack of sleep, the physical strain of hurrying to the shelter and awaiting the menacing drone of German planes and the scream of bombs somewhere near, was all too much for my poor mother and the doctor advised me to send her out of London if I could. With much heartache, it was decided to accept my older sister's invitation to have my mother and Vera with her in Long Eaton in the Midlands. It was a painful decision for us all.

On the night before they were to leave, we all went to my aunt's at Golders Green from where a car was to collect my mother the next morning. As we all gathered in her large sitting room, the siren went. For a time there was silence and my aunt asked me to play some familiar folk songs on the grand piano. The menacing sound of planes began and suddenly the whole house shook to its foundations with an indescribable jar. It was a land mine which – we heard afterwards – destroyed a whole road.

Next morning the siren went again as we waited for the car. It was too much for my mother. She had a heart attack, fortunately slight. She had asked to drive past our home once more and there I picked a bunch of her loved flowers; a sad moment, for I knew it was unlikely she would ever return. The only cheerful moment was when Vera's little dog, which was supposed to remain with me, rushed out into her arms and refused to be parted from her, barking and wagging his whole small body. I could not deny Vera her companion – Mickey became an evacuee also!

Then began a long period – until the end of the War in 1945 – when I only lived occasionally in my home and at other times stayed with friends, for it was no time to live alone. My neighbour had returned from the country, where she had been sent with a number of East End women and their children as her 'War Work'. The Eastenders had all drifted home again quite soon, 'fed up' with the country. So Una Morris took up work in the Hendon Food Office and we shared her house.

Life had a crazy routine. We went to bed, putting everything ready for a night of raids. If we were lucky, there were no alerts, but most nights we were not so lucky, so spent some time in my shelter, or in a cupboard under the stairs (known as The Hole) or, later, in the street shelter. As the planes ground over, Una (who was a Christian Scientist) would say, "This Evil does not exist. It is only Matter." I could not share this illusion. Sometimes a few fire bombs would fall and I would help to put them out with a bucket of sand – quite exciting! On my 'duty nights', I sallied forth into the streets and I and a neighbour (male) would look out for bombs. We would discuss philosophy or some subject which had nothing to do with the War. The most delightful sound was the 'All Clear'.

My mother did not survive long, dying in 1941. She, who had faced the break up of her married life at the age of fifty-three, and had worked so hard to keep herself and Vera for years, no longer had the strength to meet this new strain. I think, too, that it broke her heart to have to leave the home and garden she had loved so much, with its security and affection. We brought her home to Hendon to her last resting place.

It was a hard time for Vera, too, for she had to do some kind of War Work and this meant she could no longer live with me. She was 35 years old and chose to join a woman who grew tomatoes in Hertfordshire. Later, she worked on the land. It was too heavy work for her small, slight body, but it was congenial.

It seemed that normality had ceased and life was suspended until that longed-for day when the conflict would be over, and, on May 8th 1945, the War ended officially. It was not until August that the War with Japan ended with the terrible bomb on Hiroshima.

Now we could go to bed and sleep undisturbed. We did not hear ever again the ominous wail of the siren or the deadly advance of the flying bombs. No one who had not experienced it, could ever realise the strain of life in War conditions. It was to be a long time before we could accept any sudden explosion without a tremor of fear. Young people of today can have no conception of what it was like to live during a war.

Hendon was not an 'evacuation area', but nevertheless more than one thousand bombs of every variety had fallen on the borough. During one month alone, nearly 400 bombs had been dropped in Hendon, plus eight mines and 40 oil bombs, which make an awful stench and mess. A mine which dropped only three minutes walk away killed nearly 100 people. Lives had been lost and thousands of houses destroyed. As in all areas, work had gone on, men and women had endured fear and terror and there had been a comradeship and compassion that is all too rare in modern times. We were all in it together.

On VE Day, light streamed from open doors of every house, bonfires blazed, people sang and danced together, even in our decorous street.

Many had lost their loved ones and they were not forgotten at this time, but we could relax on this one day of peace. This was the real 'All Clear' and, for the moment, we need look no further. It inspired me to write a poem:

> There's the 'All Clear'
> Tired children heavy-eyed
> Stumble upstairs to bed. The sounds of night
> Which for long hours, a cold and menacing tide,

> Have compassed us with fear, recede again
> Into oblivion. Hearts are alive
> With hope once more, and courage conquers pain.

'So they depart, with a smile and a nod, and we miss them...' (*The Wind in the Willows*)

The War at an end, men and woman returned to civilian life and took up their posts with a sense, not only of relief, but with a hope that now they could look ahead and plan for the future in spite of the destruction.

So, in my world of libraries and books, plans were made for new branch libraries. Three such libraries were built between 1952 and 1962, and an extensive Travelling Library Service established in 1947.

These new areas of service meant increased responsibility for me. Children's Librarians had to be appointed and supervised, activities planned and a considerable number of books selected and purchased. My staff had their part in all this of course, but mine was the ultimate responsibility. I provided estimates of expenditure, wrote reports and made the necessary contact with officials and visitors who were, by then, numerous, as Hendon had won a reputation for service to children. Incidentally, it was ironical to note that I, who had often been bottom of the class in maths, could cope with the statistics, estimates, book invoices for thousands of pounds and mathematical details of my profession, quite adequately. Could this be a reflection on methods of teaching – or merely due to necessity and because I now saw the purpose of these calculations?

I still had my daily duties as a librarian and my contact with children, for this was the basis and inspiration of all my activities, whether within the library or in the outside world.

First and foremost was the selection of my stock-in-trade – books. This involved becoming acquainted with all books available, consulting publishers' catalogues, periodicals concerned with books (such as *The Junior Bookshelf*), visiting bookshops, attending exhibitions and the cocktail parties given by publishers, extremely noisy and heated affairs at which one met authors, publishers and other interesting people.

And I read and read at every opportunity, for I believed that, in order to give a good service to children, it was necessary to *know* what was in the books. My knowledge became extensive and gradually I was involved in writing about books in the journals concerned with publishing, in lecturing to many societies, colleges, at conferences and on radio and – eventually – television.

I even had the temerity to talk on books and libraries at library conferences – that last bastion of officialdom. I had become part of the revolution in the publishing of children's books. When I became a librarian in 1926, children's books had been the 'Cinderella' of publishing and it had sunk to its lowest ebb during the War, due to the shortage of paper and the limited staff everywhere. But in the period after the War, publishers appointed children's book editors and a talented number of writers and artists flourished in the children's book world. I think – looking back – that this period could be claimed as a second 'Golden Age' of children's literature, including as it did such authors as Arthur Ransome, Rosemary Sutcliff and Philippa Pearce, and outstanding illustrators like Edward Ardizzone, Brian Wildsmith, Charles Keeping and many others. A fresh wind seemed to be blowing through the children's book world sweeping away the cobwebs of the Victorian aftermath, reflecting the new conception of children in education and in society generally.

School libraries were a matter of concern in the 1950s. They were now to be established in primary and secondary schools, with a grant from the County Council. Over the years, I prepared statistics periodically to get this sum increased. The books were chosen by the teachers and I supplemented these with fiction from a central stock which was changed every year. School libraries had had a bad name because of neglect, but I found that good relations with the teaching staff and supervision did much towards banishing the sight of piles of shabby books from the corners designated as 'libraries'.

Special collections of books on specific subjects were also appreciated. Over the years, I built up a collection of pictures (which my Junior Library Helpers liked to mount, covering themselves liberally – and happily - with paste in the process). This collection grew to thousands and special storage was provided for it. Later, I was able to build up an exhibition of books which teachers could visit and from which they could make their own selection. In this, as in everything I did, my purpose was to encourage the publication of the best and most useful in children's literature. So now, Hendon had children's libraries in every branch, stocked with carefully selected books, in the charge of trained assistants and enlivened with activities of many kinds, from displays, Story Hours, clubs based on the interests of children, talks by authors and other interesting people and Book Weeks which covered the whole borough of Hendon. The children themselves were involved in everything that went on and the Junior Library

Helpers took an active interest in the library they regarded as theirs.

The Children's Library was considered to be progressive and interesting and was on the 'visiting list' of the Library Association and educational organisations, so we had visitors from overseas. Shakwantela, for instance, a charming and intelligent Indian girl, who was compiling a list of children's books for UNESCO and delighted our eyes with a different sari every day.   Then the large Nigerian who ignored all physical exertion, and the African girl who shivered all day and regarded all my efforts to teach her cataloguing with complete, good-natured, indifference.   There was the learned librarian from Jerusalem who invited me to visit him there, and the professor from Venezuela where 60% of the borrowers were children.   The librarian from Istanbul told me that there were very few books for children as they did not *want* to read anyway, and it was the librarians' job to help children with their lessons.   Grace Hallworth, who came from Trinidad, was later to make a distinguished career in England.   A frequent visitor was a nun in the attractive purple habit of a Belgian order.   Her lively personality entertained us, but we never did discover quite what she was studying.   A Norwegian visitor – in the year before the War – became a friend.   We lost sight of each other during the Occupation, but I found her again in time to become the English godmother of her only son.

Perhaps it would be of interest to describe a typical day or two in this busy life:

> H.Q.   Six branch librarians to chose books at Selection meeting.   A Danish librarian, a visitor.   Two teachers to choose books for school. Many parcels of books arrive for branches.   Books everywhere, telephone ringing.   Invoices to be checked.   My assistants with their modern education need help with ordinary arithmetic. Enquiry from BBC about an unknown book.   Storytelling session at Central Library.   Talk in evening ...   In London by 10am.   Rushed a committee through in my firm sledge-hammer manner.   Went to a Luncheon.   Came back to Chaucer House to see a librarian. Returned to Hendon to find 80 children waiting to hear a story. Examined two cubs for Reader's Badge, etc.

It might be wondered whether – with all these activities – I had time to enjoy any private life.   Of course I did, but not to the degree which is considered essential for happiness today.   I did find time for the theatre and saw most of the great actors of the day, returning home at night through London streets, which at that time offered little danger.

My family has always been my particular concern. The War had broken up my home in Hendon and my mother had died in 'exile'. Vera, having taken the totally inadequate wartime training of one year as a teacher, was now based in country towns. I eventually sold my house, with the happy memories it had known and shared a friend's home. As she was a teacher of Drama, we had mutual interests.

In 1952, she and I bought a second hand car impulsively, took the test and set out to make sallies into the country, just as, in the previous generation, women had discovered the freedom of the bicycle. At that time, motoring was a pleasurable way of seeing Britain, for there were still quiet roads and very few motorways. This first car had a leaking roof and a hole in the floor, but it held together tentatively. In the only mishap we ever had, my friend took a bend too rapidly, mounted a bank and, taking her hands off the wheel, said nervously, "Oh, what ought I to do now?"

My father had moved from his last circuit to a retirement bungalow in Cornwall. After my mother's death, he married his housekeeper, a homely, capable widow, so he was well cared for. He was too far away for us to visit him regularly and I fear he was often lonely. My father was perhaps closer to me than to my sisters and brother, for we were both 'book lovers' and wrote poetry of a kind. I owed him a great deal, for it was he who had secured me my career and it gave him a shared pleasure – and a little pride – when I was successful in any way. I did what I could for him, but it was sadly little.

My father died in 1954. Vera and I travelled down to Cornwall to attend his funeral. It was so impersonal and I felt I could not bear that this should be my farewell to a father who had always been kind and loving to me. In the afternoon I set out alone to walk to the cliff top, a journey my father and I had often shared, for he loved to walk through the countryside to the cliffs overlooking the sea. The rough country road was deserted and there was no one on the cliffs. The wind marshalled great white clouds across the sky and lashed the waves to spray; seabirds dived into the white spume at the foot of the cliffs – a day he would have enjoyed. As I stood there, alone in the wind and the rain, I suddenly felt a sense of release and knew that I need grieve no longer for him. This moment was my real farewell. This is how he would have wished it to be.

My father left behind hundreds of sermons, a book on his theological beliefs (which were unconventional and unpopular), a shorthand system which was never adopted, poems and other writings. In none of these works was he successful and he regarded himself a failure. But was he? Before all else he was a faithful servant of God and, in ministry with his people, was always sincere and compassionate. This is the real man, and my hope is that he had his reward in that other land of the Spirit.

In 1953, my brother, a widower, married my friend, who then decided to sell her house, so I moved to a flat which was my home until I retired. This enforced solitude was a blessing in disguise, for it gave me freedom for what lay before me, a period in which I was to enjoy many forays into 'foreign parts'. These were mostly on library matters – conferences for IBBY (International Board on Books for Young People), IFLA (International Federation of Library Associations) and for story-telling, my particular pleasure.

PART FOUR
LIBRARY MATTERS

CHAPTER ELEVEN

At about the age of eleven, when I realised that children were not welcomed in public libraries, indeed not always admitted, my dream of a library where children *were* welcome to borrow books - a place planned especially for them, where they could sit and read and feel free in a wealth of books - was born. So when I became a children's librarian, I welcomed all children, with their differing characteristics, from the Jewish boy who read Jane Austen to the boy who, at the age of eleven, was already a burglar and never read a book but loved to be in the library.

With the opening of the library, there was now a permanent centre where children could develop their reading tastes and grow up with books. I was very conscious of my responsibility in this to provide a well-stocked library and guidance where it was needed, for this was Hendon's first library and a new experience for the generation of children whom I welcomed in 1929. They would become the first generation of adult borrowers. I watched them with excitement and anticipation. Some day I would know these boys and girls as individuals. It is not easy to reach a relationship with children so that there is mutual trust.

One of the most interesting facets of my work has been watching the meeting between children and books. What decides a child in choosing a book to read? What would they think of the books? Had I made the right choice for each age and for such a variety of children? I looked forward to the future with some confidence, for I was prepared to learn from the children themselves. It was the beginning of a long and happy association with books and children. I could provide the books from which they would choose, but how would each make their choice? What would decide them? Can we adults ever really know what impresses a child in a book? Sometimes they do appreciate the way in which a book is written, as witness a girl's comments on 'words':

The boring words...
I heard them dragging their feet.
But when the exciting, marvellous words
Jump out, I dance and sing with them.
The boring, the dreary words
Slip back into the book. Good for them!
I like the words which liven me up.

Enid Blyton enthusiasts can grow tired of their diet: "Well, I used to be mad about her books, but now I'm not. She's not for people of my age, is she?" said a girl of ten.

A child's memory of a book seldom retains the title or even the author's name. The wanted book is often described by its colour or position on the shelf. Asked for "the book with long nails", most librarians would recognise *Struwwelpeter*, a horrific book of rhymes originally written for German children. (Parents sometimes objected to its inclusion in a library at all.) I was never able to identify a child's request for Shakespeare's 'Mixed Bluebeard'. And what about the older girl who asked for "a book to put me in a dream"?

Undoubtedly, the outward appearance of a book is important. In my childhood, library shelves had a uniform dullness because of the sombre binding in black or some dark colour. All books looked much the same. Gift books, given as prizes or for birthdays, could have some colour on their stout boards, but publishers were out to attract the adult purchaser not the child. The coming of the book jacket revolutionised the appearance and attraction of a book. Jackets could be works of art; but it was more important that they could catch the eye of a possible reader. Colour alone could invite attention. So Mary, only five, exclaimed, "I've got two books and they're both green!"

The book jacket also had the advantage of the publisher's 'blurb', purporting to be giving an idea of what the story was about – sometimes so highly coloured that the cynical adult wondered if the writer had *read* the book. Once the book was taken off the shelf, the child might sample the contents to the extent of reading the first sentence or two, thumbing through the pages. I discovered that children very seldom took any notice of an adult's recommendation, preferring to listen to a pal or follow the craze of the moment for some popular author such as Blyton, with her series and easy style of writing. (Almost every child went through a phase of Blyton, but usually grew out of it as they became more mature). Many children avoided 'history' books as sure to be dull and like school, but no-one could call Rosemary Sutcliff's historical stories boring if persuaded to try them. Naturally, most children have a particular subject in which they are interested, especially the boys. Children can become astonishingly knowledgeable on topics.

All our Library Helpers soon learned how to consult reference books of a simple kind, a knowledge which would stand them in good stead all their lives. Children can find this chasing of a certain item a fascinating game, and enjoy showing a less skilful child 'how to do it'. I am astonished to observe today how many adults find it difficult to consult a dictionary or telephone directory.

So the children's library became a busy place, with children reading, helping, occasionally playing, some chatting. In such an atmosphere discipline is no problem; although the children themselves could be very severe with each other.

A child does not naturally choose the 'highest', and I do not consider it a tragedy if children do not read the 'classics', for instance, when they are young. Our hope, as librarians, was to introduce those books which we knew could be an imaginative experience, an adventure, a stimulus, a delight. To find a way of doing this was not easy, but needed an intimate knowledge of both books and children. The books we wanted to recommend, the so-called 'better books', must be on our shelves, always available. I always considered that a librarian in a children's department should be allowed to have some period in the day when she could read as a necessary part of her working day, for it is essential for a children's librarian to know the books on the shelves and to read extensively. Unhappily, for a librarian to be seen absorbed in a book seemed to be considered a dereliction of duty! However, my staff and I read as many books as possible in our time and shared our knowledge, supplementing it with reviews from *The Junior Bookshelf* - a notable venture which originated with a bookseller, H.J.B. Woodfield, a man of imagination and shrewd foresight. The first of six annual numbers appeared in October 1936. In it, books for children from picture-book age to adolescence, were reviewed by librarians, teachers and others competent to judge their merits. The journal also included articles about authors and illustrators, awards and other relevant matters to do with children's literature. Another invaluable publication, *Growing Point*, under the editorship of Margery Fisher, appeared in 1962. Occasionally a page in *The Times Literary Supplement* or the *Publishers' Circular* would be devoted to children's books; but they did not command the vast market they do today.

I found that once I had gained a child's trust, he or she might ask "Would I like this book?" To such enquiries I would always answer truthfully, "No, I don't think so," or (sometimes artfully), "It might be too difficult for you." I usually got a truthful answer when the book was returned. Sometimes it might be "No, it was boring, I didn't finish it"; at other times, my recommendation was approved with a "Smashing!" I learned wisdom for, too often, I had seen well-meaning adults thrust a book at a child and say "This is a good book, dear. You will love it" - followed by the child's replacement of the book on the shelf when unobserved.

To match taste with book needs understanding and honesty, a recognition that a book, however well written, must have that integral quality that appeals to the child. Boys and girls can have – and express, if encouraged – very definite views about the books they read. For this reason, I kept a notebook handy in which children could write their own opinions about the book they had read. Other children would take notice of the opinions of their mates and perhaps try a recommended book themselves. So then, in this review book such informed remarks as the following:

> My chief criticism is that the same people are in book after book. She should give them a rest for a while (Boy of 13)

> These books need an author who writes in harder words to rewrite them

> If this is an example of American Literature, they can keep it

Of course, there are many ideas a librarian can use to introduce books or authors to children; for example, displays linked to a particular author, or on some chosen topic; talks by real, 'live' authors. (For some unknown reason, children imagine 'authors' to be a special kind of person, who should *look* like an author, which usually means some eccentricity of appearance or dress.) We usually planned a Reading Scheme for the Summer holidays. These were on a theme of general interest such as Space, the Countryside, Adventure. Each child had to read books from a list drawn up by the librarian, graded by age and difficulty, and had to answer questions to prove they really had read it, before progressing to a higher stage. The scheme we had in 1961, for example, was based on King Arthur, and the readers progressed gradually from the rank of 'Page', to 'Squire', 'Knight', and finally to that of 'Knight of the Round Table'. At this stage the reader designed a Coat of Arms for him- or herself, and these were displayed for everyone to see. As an ultimate aim, the reader could be a Knight of the Holy Grail, which demanded the reading of special books. The local Rotary Club on this occasion gave a Puffin Book to the winner in each grade, and a small silver cup to the reader who achieved the ultimate goal. These schemes were popular as something to do in the holiday and for the element of competition - and for the pleasure of reading, for these were the days before there were so many counter attractions such as television. Also, from the librarian's point of view, a great deal could be learned of children's views on particular books. There were always a considerable number of children who took part, for the holidays were long and this provided a purpose and a not too demanding programme of activity.

Besides these tangible methods of introduction, there was the regular Story Hour, for I regarded storytelling as an important and natural way of introducing books to children. Obviously, the folk tale was an essential part of any storytelling programme, but authors of imaginative stories could also be introduced in this way by telling an episode from a book which could be found in the library.

So we had regular Story Hours for children of seven to eleven after school hours and by this means introduced many stories and authors to countless children over the years.

In the 1960s, we adopted the American idea of holding a story-time for pre-school children. At these, we shared picture-books and simple stories with the young boys and girls and so accustomed them to using a library and regarding it as a means of enjoying books. Many of these young children soon showed a surprising individuality in their choice of books, came regularly to hear stories – and remembered them to tell their own children in later years.

CHAPTER TWELVE

Isoon realised how much more was needed for the successful running of a library than the pleasure of getting to know books. There was the daily running of the library, the planning of activities, the selection of books and the exacting task of learning how to help and get to know children. For all these daily tasks and problems a librarian who was in charge of a library needed help and training, but there was no course of training available. It would be most helpful if librarians could meet others in the same position and exchange experiences, but there was no organisation which enabled them to do so. A Circle of Children's Librarians had been formed in 1934 by an experienced librarian, Miss Hummerston of Leeds, but it had not survived, probably due to the indifference of chief librarians.

In 1937, W.C. Berwick Sayers, Chief Librarian of Croydon, suggested that his Children's Librarian Mrs Ethel Hayler and I should call a meeting of librarians interested in forming a new group. Mr Sayers knew me already and had shown a friendly interest in my progress because I had been the only student interested in children's libraries on the course on library work in University College. He was the only librarian to have provided a library solely for children, modelled on one he has seen in Amsterdam. With his support, a meeting was called at Chaucer House which was attended by seventy-six people. An Association of Children's Librarians was formed with Miss Hayler as chairman and myself as secretary. The annual subscription was to be one shilling for assistants who earned under £150 a year, two shillings annually for those with more than £150! – an indication of the level of salaries in libraries at the time.

In the first two years of its life, the Association found progress difficult. The general climate in the library world was not favourable to library work with children, although it had improved since the 1920s. Children's librarians were ill-paid and the designated post was rare (I was particularly fortunate in this respect). However, from the beginning, the Counties Libraries Section had been friendly and helpful and individual librarians were good friends. During these first years, visits were paid to various libraries, where we received generous hospitality from the staff – for example, Fulham, Marylebone and St Pancras, amongst others.

The Library Association itself, after making a vague suggestion that we might become a Section some time, was prejudiced against us as it was thought that we had political leaning towards the Left! However, we began to be recognised as a group of librarians with a specialised knowledge of books for children and our advice was invited occasionally. We actually issued two reports – in 1937 and 1939 - of our activities, and outlined our Constitution.

During World War Two, like all other associations at that time, our activities almost ceased. Members went into the Forces, had perforce to undertake extra responsibilities at home, and general conditions of life were difficult. Meetings were, at first, impossible because of the difficulties of travel – especially in London – and life was disorganised. But, after a time, it was recognised amongst our small nucleus that unless we could keep the purpose and organisation of the Association alive, it would be all to do again and we would lose the contacts we had gained.

So we had occasional meetings at some interesting library on Sunday afternoons and these were enjoyed and our membership even grew a little. As War conditions became familiar and life settled into an uneasy routine, our usefulness and activities grew, our knowledge and experience with book selection being particularly valued. Our help was sought by the Counties Section for their annual Book Catalogue in the children's book section, as also by the National Book Council. At this time, children's books were not reviewed critically, there was no training for library work, and those working with children were not consulted in any way about when such a department was to be planned.

When the War ended, it became possible to rally those librarians interested or active in work with children and to make plans for a working group of librarians. Our aim was that such a group might become a recognised part of the Library Association which could work for the welfare of those interested in work with children. The number of libraries with adequate provision for children was small, and the assistants working with children in libraries and schools had little standing and no voice in the decisions of the parent associations. However, the small number of members in the surviving Children's Book Circle worked together to attract supporters and, in 1946, the group was at last accepted officially as the Youth Libraries Group (YLG) of the Library Association.

It is not possible for me to compile a history of this group, but it gained strength and support steadily and took an active part in all activities concerned with children and books.

Since 1946, the YLG has instituted Weekend Schools or Conferences (the first was at Tring in 1951); courses to help students, a monthly news magazine, among many other activities.   The YLG now organises the selection of the Carnegie Medal and the Kate Greenaway Medal and is involved as a right in all matters concerning children, young people and books.   It is the voice and authority in its field.   It is a far cry from the lone voices of the tiny group suggested by that good friend Berwick Sayers all those years ago and that small group of loyal supporters!   I am grateful to have had some small part in that growth.

CHAPTER THIRTEEN

The awarding of book prizes has become a popular entertainment these days – the occasion of the announcement of the winner of the Booker Prize, for instance, merits betting on the result and time on television. Even awards to the authors of children's books, such as the *Guardian* Prize, have some appeal. This is partly due to greater public concern about children's reading, but also, I suspect, the monetary award involved makes such awards of more significance in the materialistic climate of today. The Smarties Award carries even greater money prizes and, therefore, presumably, greater publicity.

It is not my intention to provide a history of the Carnegie Medal, but only to comment on its early days of which I had personal experience. When the award was founded by the Library Association in 1936, there were no awards of this kind in Britain. The United States had the prestigious Newbery Medal (1921), France instituted the Prix Jeunesse in 1934. These were to be followed later by awards in Australia, Canada, Germany, Sweden and others.

It was Berwick Sayers who proposed the award of a medal for a children's book, as a means of commemorating the centenary of Andrew Carnegie, the benefactor of libraries. The idea was not received with over much enthusiasm as it was to be an award to book for *children* – libraries and books for children did not carry much priority in those days, although interest was developing. However, Berwick Sayers, always interested in the cause of books for children, foresaw that some encouragement for a better standard was timely.

A committee was therefore formed to organise the first award of a medal of 'the best book for children published in the British Empire in the previous year' (*Library Association Record*, 1937). It was not to be a monetary award – such a thing was unheard of at that time and the Library Association had no funds for such a project; the medal was to offer its own reward as a symbol of excellence, an honour to be valued by the recipient, an encouragement for the production of better books, and an indication to the general public that here was a book of high standard.

It might be supposed that a committee for selecting a book for children would naturally include someone with experience of books and children, that is, a children's librarian. This was not the reasoning of the Library Association at that time. The new committee consisted of the chairman of the Council, the chairman of the Executive Committee, the editors of the *Library Association Record* and the *Library Assistant*, and a sprinkling of chief librarians. The committee's task was to consider a list of suggestions obtained from a *limited* number of libraries. There were strange omissions. For instance, no county selected. How haphazard this method was became evident only gradually, although the first recipient of the award was above reproach, Arthur Ransome for *Pigeon Post*, a volume in the 'Swallows and Amazons' series popular at the time.

It so happened that – again on the suggestion of Berwick Sayers – Ethel Hayler, his children's librarian, and I had recently formed the Association of Children's Librarians (which eventually became the nucleus of the Youth Libraries Section of the Library Association). We were a small and modest group but were young and enthusiastic about the welfare of children's books and children's libraries, so we moved into action. With the support of my Chief Librarian, J.E. Walker, I approached the Library Association and suggested that it might be helpful to include one or two children's librarians on the committee. After considerable opposition, including the unfounded accusation by the secretary of the Library Association that our tiny association was politically motivated – Heaven forbid! - the Council agreed to the intrusion of one children's librarian on the committee. (Incidentally, the Newbery Committee in the United States at that time included 22 children's librarians). I was nominated as the first victim for this unenviable duty, a daunting task, for now I should be the target of the criticism always directed as the selectors of any choice of this kind. I must needs accept the challenge as I had headed the protest. I realised that I could have little influence, for not only was I a very junior librarian in the company of the elite, but was in the minority of one when it came to voting. Over the years, however, the Chiefs were kind and tolerant of my enthusiasms and I was to remain on the committee for many years more than was advisable.

Meetings were not well attended for the Chief Librarians tended to send in postal votes which could not be discussed. (During the War, no meetings were held at all for a time.) A list of thirty or so nominations for the Medal would be circulated to members who then voted arbitrarily for the book of their choice by post. After a protest, meetings were resumed officially, but they were seldom representative. I see that in a letter of protest (*LAR*, January 1944) – what a nuisance I must have been – I recorded the fact that at only one meeting were there enough members to discuss the list of nominations, and on several occasions only two members attended. In 1945 only twelve lists of nominations were sent in, a sign of general apathy about the award of the Medal.

With the end of the War and the gradual return of staff, the committee became more representative, although there were still obstacles to a considered choice. How could a book be discussed adequately when, in all probability, I and perhaps one or two members were the only ones who had read it? How could an unworthy choice be justified when a librarian who had read that book only was determined to push it through? On one occasion a member put forward a title that had not even been nominated and, what is more, bulldozed it through the committee to the Medal. Such a choice could scarcely be considered representative of the general opinion.

Another difficulty was the sheer number of titles sent in, as many as 50 or 60. At first, each library was allowed to nominate six titles, later reduced to three. For myself I would have preferred the nominations reduced to one, so that librarians were compelled to evaluate the books selected, but maybe that was unreasonable. As the committee became more knowledgeable, it was a simple matter to eliminate the majority of the titles on such lists and reduce the 'possibles' to half a dozen for serious consideration. Here, with my intimate knowledge of books, I did have some influence. Even today as many as 40 titles are put forward for the award. Are there really as many 'outstanding' books as this in one year? – I doubt it. Originally this lack of discrimination could have been due to lack of trained critical acumen, but surely today this is not so with the many courses of tuition in the library schools.

At first, the award was to be made to 'the best book of the year', an impossible claim for any book. In 1940 this was amended to an 'outstanding' book, a more possible goal to achieve. I think this quality could at least be claimed for the majority of books selected for the Medal over the years. In 1939 it was suggested rashly that the book selected ought to appeal 'not only to boys and girls but to adults as well' (*LAR* 1939), but the phrase was dropped. Indeed it was never seriously considered I suspect, although too often this criterion does sway the selection inevitably.

The terms of guidance for choosing the book for the award were much, as today: 'An outstanding book based upon consideration of plot, style and characterisation'. At once, practical difficulties arise, for plots are so varied and who is to say that one particular plot is superior to another? What really matters is that the plot, whatever it is, is developed with freshness from its setting and characters, rises to a climax and an ending that satisfies the reader's expectations. Perhaps after all, from the child's point of view (not always considered), the theme of the plot does not matter so much as long as it is a story which holds the attention and compels the reader to read on to see what happens.

The depiction of character, we say, should be true to life. What do we mean by this? Certainly many stories of fantasy do not resemble life as we know it, yet there is an underlying truth which we recognise, whether the characters are Borrowers or Hobbits. Every story shows the reader some facts of life, some trait of character which we can recognise as common to the people we meet in life. The books that last from generation to generation are those which introduce memorable characters – Long John Silver, Jo in *Little Women*, Toad of Toad Hall.

Style cannot be defined in the language of grammar and syntax. It is concerned with the choice of words and the way in which they are used. It can be heard by the ear and appreciated by the intellect. It stamps a book as the work of an individual whose mark we can recognise by some indefinable nuance. Even children can feel the difference between a well-written book and that of an author who uses language unimaginatively.

I feel also – although this has never been stated as a criterion – that the values of a book should always be borne in mind, for these books are to be read by boys and girls in their most impressionable years. Honesty, truthfulness, courage, kindness and love, can still be presented as an essential part of life, whatever the theme of the story or the period in which it is written. Such qualities are inherent in all 'outstanding' books for children, whether it be *Tom's Midnight Garden*, *The Lantern Bearers*, or *Watership Down*.

At first, format was of considerable importance as a criterion and there was much grumbling because the Medal was awarded to publications of the Oxford University Press ten times in fifteen years. Why should a publisher be *blamed* for keeping up a consistently high standard of production at a time when this was the exception rather than the rule? Today it is taken for granted that paper, binding, design will be of a reasonable and attractive standard. In any case, the acceptance of the paperback as a norm, has somewhat destroyed the general appreciation of those physical features which still characterise a 'real book' for older readers like myself. Format is, of course, of *essential* importance in candidates for the Greenaway Medal, for here quality of paper, print, reproduction and design is obligatory for the full realisation of the artist's artistic imagination.

All these criteria, whether consciously or unconsciously, sway the selection of any book for the award, or should do so.

It is interesting to look back over the many years at the winners and observe how they have stood the test of time. Did they really merit an award? How do they stand up to the test of quality and appeal?

In the four years before World War Two, each of the four awards had some quality that made it outstanding, and indicated the developing standard of children's books. Arthur Ransome's stories had established a new kind of holiday adventure, essentially practical in its detail and based on personal experience. Eve Garnett's *The Family from One End Street* was the forerunner of stories about working class families, told without condescension, which showed real children without the advantages of middle-class boys and girls (as seen in most stories) and yet having interesting adventures and a warm family life. Noel Streatfeild's *The Circus is Coming* was written from first-hand information, on a subject and a way of life that appealed to children. Eleanor Doorly's *The Radium Woman* was one of the first attempts to show children the excitement of scientific discovery achieved in spite of immense difficulties. All these books appealed to children, unlike many of the subsequent choices for the Medal.

Inevitably the quality and choice for the Medal declined during the War years, with the shortage of paper and materials and the absence of authors and illustrators and those concerned with children's books. For this reason, no award was made for the years 1943 and 1945. The books selected in 1940 and 1941, Kitty Barne's *Visitors from London* and Mary Treadgold's *We Couldn't Leave Dinah,* were largely topical, relating to War conditions, and had little enduring quality, I think. Eric Linklater's *The Wind on the Moon*, the first award of many made to fantasy, has not achieved the esteem of the later choices in this field. The most original and lasting of the awards made in these five years was unquestionably B.B.'s *The Little Grey Men* (1942). It came as a breath of fresh air in the darkness of the War years, a call to the elemental and enduring joys and lore of the countryside, *and* it was a book that children could take to their hearts.

The next twenty years were to show the development of many new trends and fresh approaches to older forms in children's literature. With the advent of Cynthia Harnett and Rosemary Sutcliff, the historical story gained status – and more willing readers. Cynthia Harnett's *The Woolpack*, with its meticulous detail in words and illustrations, enticed many children to visit and verify for themselves the background of the story. History became real and exciting. Rosemary Sutcliff brought an artist's eye to her vivid recreation of historical periods, notably the Roman. What is more, her storytelling talent gave new life to remote historical times. While it was her *The Lantern Bearers* which was awarded the Medal in 1959, probably her best known and loved story was *The Eagle of the Ninth.*

Some of the best writing in children's books is in the form of fantasy. The second award in this genre (after *The Wind on the Moon*) was Elizabeth Goudge's *The Little White Horse* (1946), a sensitive and imaginative story, but probably considered a little sentimental today. C.S. Lewis won the Medal with his *The Last Battle* (1956), the final volume in the series of books about the mysterious land of Narnia, stories considered by some critics to be an allegory of the Christian religion and its promise of an after life, but still enjoyed by children as good stories. Pauline Clarke's *The Twelve and the Genii* brings to life the soldiers round which the Brontë children wove so many stories, an imaginative tale which still serves as an introduction to the Brontë books. However, by far the most outstanding book was *The Borrowers*, a stroke of genius by Mary Norton.

Six of the choices are about real life, or what is called real life. Two of these - *Nordy Bank* by Sheena Porter and *The Grange at High Force* by Philip Turner - were competent tales but not, I think, sufficient to stand the test of time. Elfrida Vipoint's *The Lark on the Wing* had more enduring qualities, for the author's sincerity and principles shone through the story. *The Grass Rope* was one of William Mayne's earlier books and one of the best, with its strong feeling for 'place' and folk beliefs and the convincing characterisation. Lucy Boston's *A Stranger at Green Knowe* is the passionate vehicle for her compassion for any creature condemned to 'live on cement'. All Mrs Boston's books are individual and outstanding and nearly all are told against the background of her loved and ancient house.

In Philippa Pearce's *Tom's Midnight Garden*, fact or fantasy defies classification. It has an everyday setting but all else is out of this world and utterly convincing. A remarkable book which has become a children's classic in the author's own lifetime.

Only two awards can be called 'boys' books: Richard Armstrong's *Sea Change* and Ronald Welch's *Night Crusader*. The latter, largely forgotten, is a complex story difficult for children to understand. *Sea*

Change is written from the author's personal experience of hardship and it rings true. It is an excellent story of strength of purpose and character and it still has meaning for older boys.

The three non-fiction books chosen between 1946 and 1960, Agnes Allan's *The Story of Your Home*, I.W. Cornwall's *The Making of Man* and Edward Osmond's *A Valley Grows Up*, while interesting and outstanding in their time, have suffered the fate of most information books, having been superseded as methods of presentation as the march of knowledge has advanced. Is it really possible, in any case, to compare fiction and non-fiction or to say that in the year *The Radium Woman* won the award, that this book was 'better' than C. Walter Hodges' *Columbus Sails*, published simultaneously?

On two occasions the award was made to an author who had not produced new material in the year concerned. No apology was necessary for this bending of the rules, for the writers concerned were already established in the top rank of writers for children and had made a major contribution to children's literature. I refer to Walter de la Mare and Eleanor Farjeon. In the event de la Mare was too ill to receive his Medal in person and died shortly after. Eleanor Farjeon, too, had come almost to the end of her writing career.

In January 1944, I wrote in the *Library Association Record* that the Medal 'needs to be written and talked about, advertised in all libraries and bookshops and awarded with some ceremony'. Certainly in the earlier years this was far from the case and the general attitude of the public and the press - even of the library world - was one of indifference. The Library Association did little to publicise it, the publishers did not regard it as of much financial influence, the general public knew nothing of it. It has been known for the winning author to be astonished to receive the award as he or she had never heard of its existence. At first, the name of the winning author was kept a secret until the award of the Medal at the annual conference of the Library Association, when it was granted such a meagre allotment of time in the programme that it made little impact. A member of the Carnegie Medal committee introduced the winner in a few sentences, the President presented the Medal to the blushing recipient who was allowed to say a couple of sentences in return, little more than a courteous 'thank you'. Incidentally, the Medal itself was not always inscribed in time for the ceremony and the astonished recipient found himself in possession of a substitute medal loaned by some incongruous body such as the Fishmongers' Association. The only perquisite was a ceremonious luncheon with the President and other notables. It was not until 1954 that the Library Association agreed to hold a press conference to publicise the award and to introduce the winner as a person. Eventually it was decided that it would be fairer to present the Medal at a separate, specially organised event, so that it was not overshadowed by other ceremonies considered to be of more importance.

Perhaps the most successful and enjoyable celebration of the award was its Twenty-first Birthday Party in 1957. There was a luncheon at the Dorchester in Park Lane, to which all previous recipients of the Medal were invited. One hundred and thirty guests representing the literary and publishing world attended. I shared a table with three of the Medal winners - Eleanor Farjeon, Ronald Welch, John Bell of Oxford University Press and his wife, Pamela Whitlock author (when a girl) of a successful book, *The Far Distant Oxus*. An expensive affair, but in those days we were prepared to contribute from our own modest personal resources to make the celebration a success – which it undoubtedly was.

The Kate Greenaway Medal was instituted in 1955 to encourage the production of better illustrations and as an incentive to outstanding artists to contribute to children's books. It had been felt for a long time that the Carnegie Medal did not afford an opportunity to recognise the part the illustrator played in books for children. In reality, many artists valued the outlet children's books gave them for their talent, as the modern novel is seldom illustrated. The field for expressions of artistic experiments cannot ever be over estimated, as several artists were already proving when the Greenaway Medal was promoted. At that time Edward Ardizonne, Kathleen Hale (with her 'Marmalade Cat'), Clarke Hutton, Kiddell-Munroe and Clifford Webb were already well known for their picture books. The United States were still richer with a wide variety of artists, many from Europe as emigrants.

The first choice made for the Greenaway Medal was Kiddell-Munroe, but it was not allowed as the artist was not resident in the UK. This was a hard and fast rule - abolished in 1961, however. In 1956 the award was to Edward Ardizonne for *Tim All Alone*, a popular decision for not only were these books loved by children but Ardizonne himself had a personality which made him well loved and admired, and, because of the wide variety of his illustrations, his name was well known. Ironically, his first 'Tim' book was first published in the States and only later in this country. The list of nominations for the

Greenaway Medal numbered twenty-six, not necessarily a proof of the wealth of artistic ability in Britain, but more probably because few librarians (I was one) were qualified to judge the merits of an artist's work. Strange that there was no award in 1958, for Charles Keeping's and Kathleen Hale's names were put forward. Possibly the climate was not right for a wide appreciation of Keeping's exuberant use of colour and line. It was not until 1967 that his genius was recognised by the award of the Medal to his story *Charley, Charlotte and the Golden Canary*, and I suspect that it was the appeal of the story that swayed the decision.

Since its inception, many of our better known artists have won the Greenaway – Anthony Maitland, Brian Wildsmith, C. Walter Hodges, Victor Ambrus, Raymond Briggs, William Stobbs to mention only a few, truly a list of which we may be proud. All these choices bear out the precept that a picture book should be the creative result of imagination and that text and illustration should complement each other.

The Carnegie (and the Greenaway) is now established as a significant award, although never winning the public acclaim and interest of the book prizes which carry substantial money prizes. I still feel that the award would have been better made for the author's 'body of work' (as in the Hans Christian Andersen Award) rather than for an individual title. The latter rule has meant that many fine authors have never been recognised because they have not happened to produce a suitable book in the right year. The neglect of C. Walter Hodges, Rumer Godden, J.R.R. Tolkien, Barbara Willard and Alison Uttley, are obvious examples.

The composition of the selection committee has altered radically from the bad old days when I was the only children's librarian allowed as a member. Today, at long last, every member of the selection committee is engaged in work with children and there is a representative from each of the branches of the YLG, so that all members of the Library Association have an opportunity to express their views.

Many criticisms are made of the choice for the Carnegie Medal and this is a healthy sign for it shows there is interest in the choice made. Some say that the standard is too 'elite' and that children will not read the winning books. When I was a librarian I considered that it was my duty and a challenge to see that children were introduced to the 'Medal book' as a pleasure and privilege. Faith in the intrinsic value of such books, and a belief in the ability of many children to appreciate the best when it is presented to them attractively, can help a great deal.

Another criticism is that the books are chosen by adults without regard to the children who are expected to read them. It is certainly true that on several occasions, for instance there has been a tendency to select a book aimed at 'young people' rather than children. After all, the award was meant to be chosen for children. It seems a pity that childhood should be whittled away in this direction as well as suffering from the forces of commerce, politics and the ever present immensely powerful influence of television.

What do we expect of a Carnegie Medal book? Surely that it should be read and appreciated for many years as an example of excellence. The best books for children do not date and are kept alive by the children themselves in the only possible way – by being read.

Inevitably, the books chosen will reflect changes in social life and the influence on children's tastes in reading, and there will be departures from the original purpose of the Medal, but I hope the Carnegie will continue to be awarded. It provides a motive for the considered discussion of books. It is of the utmost importance that our books should be chosen with care – whether on library shelves or in the home. "Only the best is good enough for children," as Walter de la Mare said.

CHAPTER FOURTEEN

In July 1957 I was asked to be a member of the Hans Christian Andersen Jury. This Jury was the inspiration of Mrs Jella Lepman, who in 1952 founded IBBY. The Jury was to select an outstanding book from those submitted by the member countries. The first award was made to Eleanor Farjeon for her book, *The Little Bookroom*, in 1956. Several nations had formed a section of IBBY but England was not one of them. I had been informed by Jella Lepman that I had been elected by the Executive of IBBY to represent England. Possibly Mrs Lepman thought I was influential enough to persuade the publishers to form a British Section. In this she was mistaken.

Jella Lepman was a remarkable woman. She was German by birth, but British by naturalisation. After the war she had returned to Germany. She was shocked by the utter devastation, not only of the cities but also of German culture since the Hitler regime. The children were not only physically hungry, but bereft of books.

She set about organising book exhibitions all over Germany and these were so successful that in 1948 she established The International Youth Library in Munich with a stock of books in as many languages as she could obtain. In those early days she received valuable support and inspiration from three internationally known authors – Erich Kastner, the German author of *Emil and the Detectives*, Astrid Lindgren, Swedish author of *Pippa Longstocking* and Pamela Travers, English author of *Mary Poppins*. Her library was especially rich in picture-books, for pictures were a universal language which all children could understand. A woman of formidable will and determination, she had a gift for persuading those with riches or power to subsidise her ideas.

I was not surprised therefore when she informed me that I was to be a member of the Jury and I consented, for I admired all that she had done for books and children. First of all – with the substantial help of Mr Woodfield (founder of the *Junior Bookshelf*) we called a meeting to try to persuade the publishers to form a Section of IBBY for England. This they refused to do as they did not wish to pay the fee necessary to allow England to submit an entry for the Medal – this from a country which had a great reputation for the quality of its children's books.   Mr Woodfield, the public-spirited man, paid the subscription so that England could send an entry.

Now I was committed.   I would have to pay my own expenses for attending the Jury and use my own time, no mean consideration at that period of my busy life.

First of all I had to write to publishers and others and persuade them to submit an entry, which involved supplying a copy of the book submitted for each member of the Jury.   This was not popular!

Now books began to come to me – the entries from other countries which I was supposed to read and judge.   On one occasion they were in ten languages.   Each book was accompanied by a précis of the plot or subject in English, German and French.   Sometimes the précis was not very helpful!   For example:

> On a little town, where one could not longer be happy, an autumn day, a boy very introverted, with a small bundle on hi [sic] shoulder, accompanied by a white cat and a swallow who could not emigrate because of a broken wing, they enter into a forest...

Meetings were held in Zurich or Geneva, and lasted two or three days.   On the first occasion there were members from eight countries – France, Germany, Austria, Switzerland, Italy and the Scandinavian countries and England.   Each delegate spoke for his or her own national entry and there was a general discussion about the books.   This could be very heated and national in feeling, but was helpful in deciding the respective merits of the entries.   Mrs Lepman generally decided before-hand which country she favoured to win the Medal, so there was a great deal of argument.   It was almost impossible to have a balanced opinion of a book one could not read in the original and without knowledge of the country from which the author came.   Somehow a decision was reached which, however, was often a surprisingly good one and repre-sents the most valued authors of the country of origin.

This entry from my diary of 1964 will serve to give an impression of a typical Jury meeting.

[The Jury members were:]

Virginia Haviland (USA), very efficient and fond of statistics;
Dr Richard Bamberger (Austria), busy, energetic little man, called
Bambi by Jella; Dr Klaus Doderer (Germany), very German; Lisa
Christina Pearsson (Sweden), elegant and emotional; Bettina
Hurlimann (Switzerland), kind, in her quiet way tries to keep Jella in
order; Azeola (Spain), has fourteen children (why do I remember this
fact only?). There was also a glamorous woman from Italy and a very
Gallic Frenchman. I am not official as England has not paid the
subscription, but am made welcome and allowed to speak.

We meet in an old barn in Bettina's garden, sitting round a ping-pong
table, the net still in place as if to divide the two factions that are
always there beneath the surface. Nine countries have sent in entries.

We speak in turn, giving our votes for each candidate by symbolic
marks. This takes all morning and is followed by an interval for
bathing in the lake or just sitting in the sunshine amongst the flowers
and eating fresh cherries. A ladder against the cherry tree and we are
invited to help ourselves whenever the urge comes over us. When we
return to work Azeola sums up in French and we vote for three entries,
then two, then one. At this point we are at loggerheads over
Guillot (France) and Jansson (Finland). (Lisa says *sotto voce* that Jella is
"too old to understand Jansson"). After an interval, voting again.
Colwell who is sick of this long-drawn-out altercation, gives a down-
right speech (to her surprise) and Guillot has it. We congratulate the
French delegate who beams delightedly.

We sit by the lake to draw up the honours list and are well bitten by
Swiss midges or mosquitoes as a result. Later we sit in the darkness lit
only by a lantern on the terrace and the moon rising over the water.
Occasionally a boat floats past and the lake water ripples.

Sunday is a day of work too. Jella says to me, "To give Guillot the
Medal does not fill me with joy!" We work all morning on the
Honours list, with frequent drinks of cider as it is so hot. A Swiss
book, Hoffman's *Bilder Bibel* is suddenly added to the list (could it be
because Switzerland has increased its subscription?) "Guillot is a good
choice," says someone. "We haven't awarded the Medal to a book in
the Latin language so far ... "

I am reminded acidly that England hasn't paid its dues. I am only too
conscious of this – it is why I have to pay all my own expenses on these
occasions!

Lisa is offended with something or someone. "What is the matter, my dear?" says Jella with a crocodile smile.

Jella invites me to tea and asks me to place her latest book with an English publisher. (Embrace.)

Sweden takes me to dinner. She complains that the fruit is not fresh. "Madam," says the waiter philosophically, "it is a thing we must learn in life, that we shall be cheated..." This does not go down well with Lisa.

Bambi arrives and takes me to the station in a taxi very kindly – he is a good-natured, cheerful man with an excellent business sense. I discover that I am a day late for my 'plane by some travel agent's error. However, a seat is found for me on another 'plane. I reach home at 4:30am having picked up my car at the airport. At 7:30 I get up again to go to work.

I was an unofficial member representative of Britain on the Jury from 1957 and I resigned in 1964. I felt I had done my share to keep the door open for a future Section for England. It was not until some years later that a Section was finally formed and it lasted for twenty years, but was then dissolved for financial reasons and lack of interest by publishers and others.

I had become very dissatisfied with IBBY and the Jury. I feel there is too much political bias which can prevent an excellent book from being elected. Also the Jury is not very efficiently run. While its aims are excellent and I admire and support them, it is not really practicable to judge books in this way and to pronounce one book or the work of one author better than any other in a different country. As I say, how can we assess the literary value of a book if we cannot even read it in its original language? How can we evaluate the ideas and values of a book while knowing little about its background? At best the judgement we make can only be an arbitrary one.

I do not regret the time and money I have spent as a member of the Jury for it has been a valuable experience and I have met and made friends with many people from other countries. It has been a privilege – and I owe it to Jella Lepman that inspired and compassionate woman who has achieved so much for children and books. I have often been embarrassed by her demands but I am glad I have been involved with her aim.

*   *   *   *

I have always enjoyed travel and so I was grateful for the opportunities my profession gave me to attend international committees in other countries.   To represent Britain brought me many friends and enabled me to see much of interest abroad, but the most enjoyable part of these journeys was their aftermath – a few days with a friend travelling to wherever we chose.

Virginia Haviland, Director of the Section for Children's Literature of the Library of Congress, planned our route, I booked hotels and transport and we set off 'foot loose and fancy free'.   These expeditions were relaxed and completely enjoyable for we were good friends, always compatible.

We avoided the restriction of joining a party, chose modest hotels, travelled by local transport so we saw something of the everyday life of the people, and we walked as much as possible so that we could find our way wherever we might be – in Rome or Athens and beside Lake Lucerne.

Virginia was an indefatigable traveller, equipped with guide book and camera in case we missed something.   I was less conscientious and more enjoyed odd details and funny sights such as an unexpected Punch and Judy show in a corner of ancient Rome.

There was so much to see which we had read about and met in books.   Now it took shape and substance in Delphi or as we floated down the Rhine or listened to music in ancient Dubrovnik or in Yugoslavia.

We duly visited art galleries, cathedrals, mountains and lakes.   All these had their interest, but it is individual glimpses that remain indelibly in the memory.   Of all these, perhaps the first sight of the olive groves stretching toward the dark blue Mediterranean Sea above Delphi, temples and mountains behind us in the early morning sunlight is a treasured memory.   I saw also apple blossom beside the dark fjords of Norway and the ancient churches and the dusty road out of Assisi leading down to the Convent where St Francis and St Clair would meet, the brown fields still ploughed by monks and patient oxen.

Sometimes there were emergencies, of course, as when Virginia arrived without a Visa in Yugoslavia and we feared deportation!   Or when we wandered the streets of a naval port at midnight with no hotel – ours had been closed due to bankruptcy.   A kindly Italian landlady sheltered us, forlorn and weary, in the attic of her back street hotel.

Years afterwards, we discovered that we were known to our colleagues as 'Two little ladies trotting through Europe'!

*   *   *   *

The International Federation of Library Associations was founded in the 1920s, enlisting fifteen countries as members by the 1930s. Its most valuable achievement was the publication of documents concerning library matters. The advent of the Second World War slowed down its progress but, fortunately, its secretariat was in Switzerland, so it survived. After the War was over the federation began to spread again, due to the work of individuals, especially Lionel McColvin of England. It is now world wide, an influential association in the library world.

IFLA is not in any sense a government department. It is supported by the subscriptions of its members, national and private. It is divided into sections, each representing a different type of library or library activity. Hence our own section for Library Work with Children. Each section has its own officers and organises its own activities such as seminars and conferences. Delegates pay their own expenses and attend conferences and other activities in their own time. The federation has given valuable service to libraries and books for many years. One wonders whether it would have called forth such selfless service had it been a Government department?

In 1954, Lionel McColvin, Chief Librarian of Westminster, and a prominent figure on the International Federation of Library Associations, asked me to attend the IFLA Conference in Brussels (Belgium) in 1955, to represent England in a proposal for a section of IFLA for Library Work with Children. The proposal for such a section had been put forward by Mrs Hanni Woolff of The Hague. At that time, the emphasis was on the international exchange of books and their provision for children. We agree on a Resolution on these lines, but can find no office to make copies *"C'est impossible!"* they all say to me when I boldly demand this necessary business.

There were representatives of Switzerland, Germany, Denmark and Holland. The librarian of Paris, Mlle Gruny of L'Heure Joyeous, was particularly excitable, reiterating *"le pays undeveloppe"* in every lull. At the height of this 'conference', someone asked despairingly "What do our English and American friends think?" It seemed that the USA and England had considerable prestige in the library world. At last order was restored. At this first meeting, it was not easy to surmount the barrier of language and rather vague, if sound, suggestions of principle and concerns which might be undertaken. Obviously we were all united in our concern that books of quality should be available for children in all our countries and that a library for children should be an integral part of all libraries in every country. This was certainly not a case in Europe and certainly still less so in *'le pays undeveloppe'* whose plight particularly troubled Mlle Gruny.

We held several meetings in that wet week. Virginia Haviland and I soon joined forces for, as less excitable people (although just as concerned) and speaking in a language known to some degree by all members of the committee, we were able, sometimes, to produce a clear statement.

Eventually, a list of topics – mostly about book supply – was compiled for comment by all the countries represented.

At the final assembly it was declared that the Section on Library Work with Children was now an official part of IFLA.

At the second meeting of the section, as part of the IFLA Conference in Paris in 1957, I presented a memorandum from the Youth Libraries Group of Britain. Various suggestions for the projects were put forward, including one that there was a need of well written books about the life of children from other countries, written by a native of that country. Mlle Gruny rose to the attack – by this time a number of delegates had departed in search of champagne at the reception. Mlle Gruny stated passionately that books of this kind were already existing – it was only necessary to think of that wonderful book, *The Wind in the Willows*, to know what life was really like in England. At this statement, the rest of the audience 'softly and silently vanished away' and I was left to cope with the problem.

At the preliminary meeting at Lund in Sweden, , in 1960, it was proposed that I should be chairman for the coming years. I was reluctant because of my various commitments and I thought Mrs Bredsdorf would make a better and more experienced chairman.

When Mrs Wolff, in her last year as chairman, told the meeting that it was proposed that I should supersede her, uproar ensued for, apparently, such a matter should be put forward by Mr McColvin and, as he was not present, I could not be chairman. Mr Hutchings, although he did not approve of children's librarians, kindly came to our rescue. Surely Mr McColvin had a representative at the meeting? Had he any objection to Miss Colwell being elected as chairman? "None at all," he said. So I became chairman! It did not appear that it would be an enviable post. To my astonishment, the meeting applauded the decision and the formidable Dr Gelderblom said kindly, "Do not worry. We will help you!"

We dispersed full of good intentions about our future plans for action. We must be *seen* to do something. How thankful I was that I had such an excellent supporting committee. Annie Moerkercken, from Holland, was to be my secretary and I had every confidence in her efficiency.

My first period as chairman of the Section on Library Work with Children was at the IFLA Conference at Edinburgh in 1961. A large number of delegates attended our meeting, although there was another session at the same time. Our speakers were a success, especially elegant Mrs Schildt of Sweden, who represented the publishing angle and sang a nursery rhyme, surely the first time such a thing had been done in the history of the IFLA. Mrs Aase Bredsdorf, a pleasant Danish woman, was both charming and practical, and reassured the meeting about our progress and future plans.

After this good beginning, it seemed a pity that Mr Hutchings should choose to speak at length about the dishonesty of children's librarians who all selected the books they liked rather than those children liked. I treated this in the way it deserved – as a joke – and the audience responded.

The executive meeting was very tedious, and Mr Hutchings very sensibly slept through most of it. Thus ended my duties as chairman on this occasion and it only remained for me to attend the splendid reception at the Castle where I danced in a stately fashion with the Finnish delegate I had met on the plane.

At Berne in Switzerland in 1962, I stated that we were planning a volume containing fifteen accounts of library work with children in other countries, edited by myself. We hope to produce this for the next conference. This was to be followed by further publications on various subjects connected with libraries and books. The delegates, fired with enthusiasm, suggested other directions for our industry as, for instance, a list of sources for criticism of books for children and prizes awarded for children's books.

The meeting was pronounced 'the clearest and most concrete of all at the conference' and I was complimented on my chairmanship, but I felt that much credit was due to my exceptionally able committee,

Berne was a beautiful setting for a conference and now we could enjoy it. The historic city with its arcades and churches and chiming bells, was fascinating. In the evening it was delightful to relax and watch the sun setting over the distant mountains.

An enjoyable conference made so by a good will and a sense of achievement and the thought of all we might be able to do in future.

The journey to Sofia in Bulgaria, the 1963 venue, was via Vienna and it began unfortunately for Virginia Haviland for, by some official error, there was no seat available on the plane from Vienna to Sofia. Instead she had to travel on the railway for 24 hours and there was no food available!

The journey by air was not enjoyable either, for the plane was cold, the weather stormy and, at one point over the mountains, the plane dropped fifty feet. Passengers and staff suffered!

We were welcomed warmly at Sofia, although no one could speak English or our respective languages.

In the hotel almost everything need repair – my bathroom, for instance, was flooded permanently, every clock was stopped and the lift was perilous. There was little traffic on the wide streets, for private citizens were not allowed cars.

Virginia did not arrived until midnight of the second day. At the same time we were awakened by the sound of marching feet, shouted military orders and the rumble of tanks. The authorities had omitted to inform the visitors that this was a rehearsal for the National Day.

Our section's first meeting was difficult for I found that it was impossible to keep to the programme we had planned because of the language difficulty. So I enlisted the help of anyone had had a little knowledge of Russian (which was sometimes understood by the Bulgarians) and with everyone translating from language to language, we had a little, if confused, discussion and exchange of ideas and there was good will. For the second important meeting I looked for an interpreter. After much visiting of officials, I found a lively young Russian and we were able to say something about our work and plans for the future. Our first publication on Translation had had to be reprinted. *Library Service to Children* had been published at Lund and we had various other work in progress. The meeting went well except that a Russian delegate insisted on reading a long paper on Russian libraries which had to be translated paragraph by paragraph and contained stultifying statistics. I realised that this delegate had been instructed to deliver the paper, or else..! It was not politic to refuse.

We visited children's libraries. We found that the scope of books for children was small because of censorship. There were libraries but no full-time assistants to work in the children's department. The young assistants questioned us eagerly about life in the West, "Do not forget us!" they begged, "Keep in touch and tell us what is happening in your country."

In the times between meetings, we visited a collective farm – a primitive way of life – an ancient monastery in the mountains, a new and vast reservoir and so on. Women were cleaning the streets, watched over by the police, that hotel was not over-clean and the food uninviting.

We were given a concert before we left. There were thrilling folk dances in national costume and a magnificent choir of quite elderly men with voices as good and well trained as in opera. It was evident that, whatever the politics, the spirit of the people had not been destroyed.

On the last day, I read my report, although I doubted the delegates from Bulgaria and Russia understood much of the proceedings. I doubted also if they would see much of me as the reading desk was so high! I spoke into a microphone and hoped for the best.

Before leaving Sofia, I visited the cathedral once more to hear again the thrilling chanting of the choir there. Standing in the vast and echoing nave – there were no seats, so old people 'sat by the wall' – I listened to the unseen voices. There was the real and enduring spirit of the people.

In Rome in 1964, a paper was given on Library Provisions for Children in Italy. It was a depressing picture, for young people had to be fourteen before they were allowed to read books in the reading room – if there was one. Over that age, they could borrow books, but mainly the only source of books was the school. Publishing of children's books was chiefly of translation of the classics and the stories of Disney films. The famous artist Bruno Munari of Milan, for instance, was not published in his own country. There were two 'Summer Libraries' in parks during school holidays. I visited one of these and found all the books were wrapped in brown paper, a depressing sight. There was no Training Course for librarians of any kind. Here, evidently, was a country which needed help and advice and influence in 'high places' to provide the necessary funds.

However, our committee was able to report progress elsewhere. Our first publication was reprinted and the *Library Service to Children* was to be revised and have a second volume. A Bibliography of sources of information about children's books, book prizes and, indeed, any useful information available about children's books was to be made. No new projects were suggested at the meeting but there was plenty for us to do before the next year's conference.

As I wrote my chairman's report, I wondered unhappily about the children of Italy. Surely they needed and wanted books as much as our own children in our own countries? How could such a country as Italy, steeped in learning and tradition, neglect its children so? We must do what we could as a Section, even though this was not regarded as one of 'les pays undeveloppe'.

Helsinki, 1965, was to be the last year of my five years as chairman. It was very cold, for Helsinki is the same parallel as Siberia. The sea is never far away – and neither is Russia, a fact of which we were very aware.

The hotel was all that Bulgaria had not been and food, especially at receptions, was ample, always a welcome adjunct for hungry and impecunious delegates!

Our first meeting was very well attended. I conducted it with my usual despatch, reporting that we had produced a publication for four years in succession and had plans for further volumes. Our reports were being reprinted and had been well received and reviewed. I then announced my retirement as chairman, as my five year term had ended. Annie Moerkercken also resigned as secretary and we named Aase Bredsdorf as chairman (Denmark) and Lisa Christina Persson (Sweden) as Secretary and they were accepted by the meeting. I remained a member of the committee.

At the reception, I was complimented on my chairmanship and one delegate remarked that he "would have been much more willing to attend meetings at IFLA if they had been as efficiently run as was our section". Another said that our Section's meetings were the most entertaining and productive than any others. At least we could claim to have been *seen*, as Mr McColvin had said at that first meeting in Paris.

In Finland, my reputation was such that I was asked to chair the Hospital Section's meeting. I did so but, as I knew nothing about the agenda, I cannot have been much good. The libraries of Finland were well organised and well used. The librarians were friendly and the book supply generous. Children's books comprised many translations, including – to the disapproval of the Americans – *Uncle Tom's Cabin*.

At the final banquet, I was placed amongst the VIPs and invited by Sir Frank Francis to visit him at the British Museum. Our section was now recognised.

And at the final assembly, I determined that at least the voice of our committee should be heard - I doubt that it was *seen*, for I was almost invisible behind the high reading desk.

After completing my five years as chairman, I continued attending the IFLA Conference whenever I could. The most valuable work of the Committee on Library Work with Children was the collecting of information about work with children in libraries in all its aspects, together with the survey of the publishing of children's books. This meant contacting many countries and finding the right person with whom to correspond, editing the information obtained and arranging for its publication and dissemination, a time-consuming process. For instance, the volume on *Library Service to Children,* and its revision and second volume, was the work of Mrs Persson and myself for five years. This was only one of the many publications compiled by the members of our committee and earned us gratitude and appreciation from the library world and a feeling amongst the children's librarians in many countries that help was available even in the most undeveloped countries of the world.

I devoted my leisure time for five years to my duties as chairman of the Committee concerned with library work with children. International work is not easy because of the difficulties of language, personalities and such varying backgrounds and standards. To bring together individuals needs patience and tolerance, but it is very unrewarding. The women who formed our committee, each distinguished in her own country, taught me a great deal and brought lasting friendship. Here we were, representatives of Sweden and Denmark, Holland and the United States and England, linked together by a common aim, to bring children everywhere the pleasure and boon of the best possible books in their respective language. This was the dream that united us.

PART FIVE

STORYTELLING
- ON THE AIR AND OFF;
FRIENDS AND PIONEERS

CHAPTER FIFTEEN

Throughout our lives we enjoy listening to stories. It is a natural instinct to want to know 'what happened next?' whether the story is real or imagined. Ever since men and women gathered in communities, there have been individuals who were able to tell stories, either by word of mouth or in books or by the means of our modern inventions, for the pleasure of the people. There is no land in the world without its fund of traditional stories which were passed on from age to age. Countless generations of children have demanded "Tell me a story!"

The history of stories and storytelling would fill many books. Reference to these storytellers can be found through the ages, lively men and women with the gift of imagination and skill with words that make the story live. They had many names – bards, shanachies, minstrels and many more. In ancient times they were the companions of kings, men of repute. There were poets, too, as for instance, Taliesin, who lived in 6th century in Wales. Homer sang and recited his *Iliad* and *Odyssey*, those marvellous tales of adventure. There were women storytellers too. It is recorded that Edward I had two storytellers at his Court, Matilda Makejoye and Pearl in the Egg. It was natural in those days before the invention of printing to sing or recite the old stories and the deeds of heroes and so preserve them for posterity, so we can still hear of the deeds of an Anglo-Saxon hero, Beowulf.

It has been said that 'as the world widens, the imagination dwindles'. If this be true, how important that children should have such a stimulus as storytelling, for we need imagination. Without, we are shut away in our own narrow environment with no 'magic casements' through which to see the other world which can enrich our lives. A child once said to me "The scenery on telly was not as good as it was in the book..." A revealing comment. All great discoveries begin in the imagination and a child is deprived indeed if he never experiences it.

People often question the need to tell stories rather than read them aloud. I have told stories to many kinds of audiences and I know by experience how different in their impact the two methods are. In *telling* a story, we establish a direct relationship with the audience, eye to eye, an unbroken sharing which is not nearly so close in reading, for the print must be followed, the pages turned, and so on.

From the earliest days of my service in Hendon, I had instituted story-telling for the children. Stories and the finding of stories to tell and to make my own, has been my joy all my life. In stories, I forget myself and am transported to magical realms of wonder. I am moved by them and so, therefore, is my audience. For storytelling is a two-way process: there is mutual giving and receiving and a harmony which is delight. The sharing of stories has been the basis of my happy relationship with children and adults alike. All the stories I have made my own are still there somewhere in my memory. Storytelling has been the bright thread running through my life, whatever my circumstances. It has brought me many friends, notably those 'bright spirits' John Masefield and Eleanor Farjeon. I have had a happy life – much of it due to storytelling.

There is a wealth of stories for 'middle-aged' children, as Americans call the tens to twelves. Older children are supposed to be too old to enjoy stories, but, with the right choice, this is not so; I have watched such an audience listen spellbound to Dickens' *The Signalman*, for example. Books and stories – well chosen – are a rich stimulus for children, for they enjoy stories. One has only to watch their utter absorption as they listen and observe the sigh of contentment as it ends satisfactorily, to know all is well, that this was the right story. Once, after I had told a particularly 'good yarn', a boy in the group jumped up and shouted "Three cheers!" and the whole group joined in, to the surprise of their teachers. We may think, sometimes, that our stories are forgotten as soon as told, but I have been a storyteller a long time and I know that this is not so. I have been told by adults that they remember a particular story and now they are telling that same tale to their own children "because it is so good".

Nowadays, children seldom listen without visual aids, teachers complain that it is difficult to teach pupils to concentrate without them. This is not surprising when so many young children are left in front of the television without the response of the parent as a stimulus.

If we can win a child's attention by a story without its visual support, it must surely help them to concentrate and use their own taste and judgement. To hear a story told necessitates concentration. To share a story in all its moods, is to establish a relationship between storyteller and child which is one of enjoyment and relaxation.

Two storytelling occasions which deserve more detailed description stand out in my memory.

In 1956, I was invited to take part in a Storytelling Festival in the USA. This was due to the friend I had made at the IFLA Committee in Brussels the previous year. Virginia Haviland was then the Reader's Advisor for Boston Central Library, a children's librarian already known in the profession. So I was granted special leave to accept this request.

This was my first visit to the States and I was able to see a number of libraries and observe their work with children, visiting Boston, New York, Baltimore and many more and meeting children's librarians and authors, a wonderful opportunity – the first of many visits abroad.

The American Library Association Conference that year was in Miami Beach in California, a tourist city, bright with tropical flowers and trees and crowded with opulent hotels. The heat was intense, almost unbearable outside the air-conditioned buildings.

The Storytelling Festival lasted for three days and was organised by Eulalie Steimmetz Ross of Cincinnati. Each storyteller chose a story to pay honour to a librarian, author or storyteller of distinction.

The standard of telling, the variety of styles and material, made the occasion memorable and every gathering was full, four hundred people. The setting was fantastic, held in the supper room of an hotel. The seats were at different levels, rising to quite a height and ending in a bar. We storytellers stood in the well on the dance floor and were warned to stayed away from the chalk marks on the floor so that we did not get out of range for the microphones. Every day, fresh flowers ornamented the room – oleander, hibiscus and seagrape.

It was a memorable occasion, enjoyed by storytellers and audience alike. I told Eleanor Farjeon's *Elsie Piddock Skips in her Sleep* and spoke two greetings, one from Eleanor Farjeon herself, the other from John Masefield; both sending blessings to this gathering to celebrate storytelling the world over.

For years afterwards, I would meet librarians who had been present and who remembered the dream figure of Elsie Piddock, one hundred-and-nine years old, 'skipping, skipping, skipping in her sleep'..

In 1961, John Masefield asked me to deputise for him at the first of the storytelling festivals he had endowed at the Boys and Girls House at the Toronto Library. It was a week of intense activity. Fortunately I was well prepared, and experienced, for such an occasion. I met all kinds of people, an interesting and enjoyable experience. I lectured at the university and gave talks to all kinds of societies and groups; was interviewed on radio and television and by the press, and told stories to hordes of children in schools and libraries, often to groups where many nationalities were represented, for Toronto is home to immigrants from many nations. I was amused to find myself described in the press as 'a small woman whose stature seemed to increase as she told the loved stories'. Others spoke of my 'laughing eyes and my dramatic voice and the way in which I made stories 'live''. Well well, was this really me?

Listening to storytellers in Toronto was very enjoyable for the stories were so varied and the storytellers so individual. In those days, storytelling was rare in England, so I listened with attention, for I had much to learn. One occasion however I treasure as a storyteller, for such an experience is rare. Again, I had told Eleanor Farjeon's *Elsie Piddock Skips in her Sleep* to an adult audience. As I said the last sentence of that haunting story and left the tiny bent figure 'skipping, skipping, skipping in her sleep', there was a dreamlike silence and stillness before the audience stirred and returned to everyday life. Such is the power of a story...

I returned, enriched with a unique experience which I could now share with John Masefield. I wish he could have heard these gifted storytellers, for listening and telling stories was always a joy to him, and he believed that, for children, "lovely stories are as necessary as pure air".

When I came into librarianship, storytelling had almost died out in the library world. I was able to share in re-establishing it again. There is a resurgence of storytelling in the community. Our multi-ethnic society is strongly involved with new stories and the traditional gift of storytelling. In 1994, a society – the Society for Storytelling - was formed and I, as the 'Grandmother of Storytelling' (a title of which I am proud) was made Patron. It represents the many storytellers who are now active all over the country, telling stories in everyday venues such as village halls, public houses, schools and in each others homes.

Recently a college in East Sussex included in its programme a course in 'Storytelling in Organisations'. The aims of such a course were stated thus:

In today's marketplace our humanity seems to be constantly undermined by ruthless competition and a soulless working environment. Now, more than ever, we need to transform the spirit in which we work. This is some-thing for which the business world currently has little vocabulary, but reach for a story and the language you need is there.

Time will show the outcome from this rather unusual alliance.
Whatever happens in the approach to storytelling in the new century, once thing is certain, stories and the telling of stories will not die.

*   *   *   *

Storytelling, as I have said, has always played an important part in my life, and in 1956 it introduced me to a new interest: the writing of books.

I had never thought of myself as a writer. My work, which included the writing of critical reviews and occasional articles and the composi-tion of reports and official correspondence, did nothing to encourage imagination. Besides, I had written so many well-written, imaginative books that it did not occur to me to produce one of my own. However in 1956, Nelson commissioned a book from me, in a careers series for girls. So I wrote *How I Became a Librarian*, the first of my twenty-five books. Surprisingly this modest book, which told of my early struggles to establish a children's library system and to further the cause of chil-dren's literature, was adopted in several countries – Holland, for instance - as an 'inspiring book' for young librarians. In Japan it was translated by Momoko Ishii and eventually became an official publica-tion of the Japanese Library Association. Its influence is shown by the following comments from Japanese librarians, of both public and bunku libraries:

> ...we will make efforts for the Japanese children's libraries to develop, remembering your struggles and your achievements. Your story will be of great encouragement to us. Thank you Miss Colwell. Thank you indeed. (1968)

> The book is never out-dated after these years and offers good reading to contemporary readers. (April 1995)

> ...This book made me aware that [a] librarian's job calls for plenty of study and love. (1995)

> [The] Children's Room in our neighbourhood is equipped with [a] fair

amount of books and staff...but I don't find any librarian who receives[s] children warmly and introduce[s] them to good books like Miss Colwell did...This is the book which all the librarians should read.

My next book was suggested by my friend Eleanor Graham, the founder of Puffin Books. It was to be a collection of stories and poems suitable for young children, based on my knowledge of storytelling.

Here was the kind of book I *could* produce with confidence from my practical experience of telling stories and so successful were the collections I made that they reached the million mark in sales in the 1980s. I followed these with hard-backed collections for older boys and girls in which I included notes on how to tell the individual stories. These anthologies included unfamiliar stories which I had discovered in my extensive reading. For traditional tales, I retold stories I found in old books in the Folklore Library.

In 1980 came my practical book *Storytelling* (revised edition 1991, Thimble Press) which was translated into Japanese in 1995, together with several of my collections of traditional material.

A unique and delightful experience was the writing of a monograph on Eleanor Farjeon. I needed bibliographical details of her many books and we spent happy hours verifying these in her early books, for each of these brought me entertaining anecdotes of her life. She refused to read the book until it was in print, for she said it was "my book", but it pleased her and many of her friends received a copy for Christmas!

The writing of my books has filled many happy hours for me. I have written only a few original stories, but perhaps I can claim an ability to edit/put together interesting anthologies of stories. The making of such books has given me many happy hours and brought me new friends. I like to feel that I have given pleasure to countless children.

CHAPTER SIXTEEN

In my childhood radio and television had yet to be invented. Our only means of visual entertainment was the magic lantern, through which a series of crude pictures on glass slides were projected on to a screen and moved manually. We were fascinated by the illusion of movement. In our case, this treat came through the auspices of the Band of Hope, a temperance movement which aimed at preventing us from becoming drunkards when we grew up. I signed the pledge many times when I was ten or so.

Radio ('wireless', as it was then called) as a means of transmitting news had been discovered early in the century, but it was to be a long time before it was available to the general public and an accepted part of life. However, by 1928 when I was in Hendon preparing my children's library system, 2LO, as it was called, was established at Savoy Hill.

I had always told stories, so I ventured on a course of tuition to improve my skill as a storyteller. I chose a teacher called Sterling Mackinlay, a former actor whose sister, Jean Sterling Mackinlay, organised charming Christmas entertainments for privileged children. I had been to one of these and heard the actor Harcourt Williams tell stories in a way that charmed me and fired me with a desire to improve my own telling.

However, when I saw my teacher for the first time, he said to my astonishment, after I had told a story, "You don't need me to tell you how to tell a story – you know how – but I can help you with voice production". This he did most professionally, and after that we enjoyed my stories together for the whole course. As a result of his tuition, I have always been able to make myself heard and talk for lengthy periods without strain.

Sterling Mackinlay thought I might well find of place for my story-telling in the new medium, radio. So he procured an audition for me through his sister and I presented myself at 2LO.

It was terrifying experience. I was taken into an empty studio, which was in darkness with only one winking red light. The producer departed and a ghostly voice said "Begin". I began to tell what I now considered to be a stupid story. I had been told to imagine the children who would be listening so eagerly to me. All I could think of was my terror of this empty studio and the machine which was recording my inane story. I was not at all surprised when the BBC politely refused my services. I was to record many programmes in the future, but never again in such an intimidating atmosphere.

After this discouraging experience, I thought no more of radio as a medium for my storytelling. I had real live children enough in my library and it was far more pleasant to tell stories to live children whom I could see.

My next experience of broadcasting was a much happier one. It was in 1944. I was asked to record a message to the children of America in a programme called 'Junior Bridge Builders'. I wrote my own script which to my relieved surprise was pronounced "charming and most moving". I had written it from the heart in a time when everyone was emotionally moved. It contained a sentence which brought home the war conditions in British libraries: "Here in England libraries are short of almost everything – staff, books, accommodation – everything in fact, except borrowers!"

(On this occasion, T.S.Eliot, the poet, recorded a far too long talk on a separate tape. Had the children to listen to this? I hope not.)

About the same time I took part in a dialogue with English children at the National Book League. We talked about books quite creditably, but the producer had had the bright idea that we should include tongue twisters, for fun. This proved disastrous and the broadcast was rescued with difficulty from unrehearsed laughter. This was a programme for 'Pen Pals in America'. There was a scheme at this time called 'Books Across the Sea' which linked children and libraries in England and the States.

During the next decade or so, I was to broadcast many times, chiefly in educational programmes, often to countries overseas. I remember one occasion for the West Indies, when I had to answer fifteen questions in a dialogue with an excitable educator from that country, after which I was invited to spend a period in the West Indies.

'Storytelling' was often my theme when I broadcast. On one occasion I had six recordings in one day, which included three stories, a talk and an interview. This was for Fernand and Anne Renier who had the largest collection of children's books in the world (now in the Museum of Childhood at Bethnal Green). On another occasion I broadcast to Europe on storytelling. There were also engagements with local radio stations.

I met many interesting people when broadcasting. I frequently shared a programme with Noel Streatfeild, elegant and sophisticated and kind, and Edward Blishen, very knowledgeable about books and stimulating as a colleague.

Only once did I have the salutary experience of 'drying up'. It was on Lionel Gamlin's live unscripted programme in company with children. We all became speechless and had to be rescued.

I always wrote my own scripts for I knew exactly what I wanted to say and it was good practice for the writing I was later to do on children's books and other relevant subjects. I was fortunate in that I had a clear resonant voice which I could use professionally – thanks to Sterling Mackinlay. I am told that my voice gave the impression of coming from a large person, so when people met me, my small stature was a surprise.

My first appearance on television was in 1948 when I was asked to talk on Librarianship as a Career on 'Women's Hour'. BBC headquarters were then at Alexandra Palace. The conditions there and the technical equipment used would now be considered archaic.

When I arrived on the day, everything seemed to be in hopeless confusion. The sets for the various items of the programme in the afternoon were grouped round the battery of cameras. My small spot contained a table (borrowed from Hendon Library), a bookcase - empty of books - and no chair. When I asked the property man for books, he produced a strip of book spines with no books behind them and some telephone directories. Fortunately I had brought a few attractive books with me.

A vague woman producer called Jean, drifted in and said she would ask me leading questions when we were on the air.

The items for the programme were being set up. There was a cookery demonstration with clattering saucepans, and two sisters were practising incessantly on two pianos. The wife of an MP was to demonstrate the ways in which women carried their babies in other parts of the world. She pestered all and sundry with agitated questions. I read through my script, most of which I had now forgotten. Lights flashed, property men moved furniture, loud speakers boomed – all seemed chaos.

In my corner I tried to work out the best way to display books for the camera. I now had a chair on which to sit – I had refused a kindergarten chair a few inches high; I hoped we would get something to eat before the afternoon. (Eventually we did – of a kind.)

Now the tension increased. An African woman appeared, to help demonstrate how babies were carried in her country – in a basket apparently. Another woman from Ecuador - whose name sounded like 'Slinky Lee' – joined her. Inexplicably, the producer pronounced her long native skirt to be "old-fashioned"; a short skirt would look more "foreign". The cookery experts clattered their saucepans. Would there ever be order?

Suddenly the lights come on, a battery of cameras gets into position and someone says "Action!" It is time!

The programme moves on through its items...

The wife of the MP is so pleased with her item that she does not want it to end. She stays on, beaming, and the stage manager has to crawl across the cables, taking care to keep below camera level. He tweaks her skirt to persuade her to move but she ignores him and the cameras have to be moved to wipe her from the screen.

Now it was my turn. I give a last look at my script and then walk on. Jean comes on and introduces me, and I look pleasant (I hope). Jean asks me an entirely new leading question, making my script useless. It continues to be so as she thinks up new variations. I struggled on and at last Jean delivers her final sentence. "Did you know," she says brightly to her unseen audience, "that the National Central Library has 20 million books? Isn't it amazing?" It was certainly amazing, and entirely untrue. I try to look pleasant as we walk off the set, but I don't feel pleasant.

Afterwards the stage manager says, to my relief, "Grand! It came over wonderfully". Someone who has seen the programme comments "It sounded as though it came from the heart – not like a script, but so natural". Well, I had been forced to abandon my script. Is this a hint for the success of future broadcasts?

In the mid-60s two new programmes for children were to be introduced: 'Play School' and 'Jackanory'. 'Play School' was to be for children of two to five years of age and 'Jackanory' for older children.

Joy Whitby, the producer of 'Play School', asked me to be a consultant on the programme because of my knowledge of children's books and my experience of storytelling and children.

At this time, the provision of nursery schools in England was very inadequate. 'Play School' was to be the 'Nursery School of the air', a daily feature of life for young children in the home. It would provide stimulation and simple instruction and entertainment for a neglected strata of the population. 'Play School' was to last for twenty years, before being drastically re-planned to satisfy changing social trends and a demand for a more sophisticated generation.

For 'Play School', I have to record five stories in one morning. This is no easy task. It means a great deal of preparation, for I must know my stories so well that nothing can 'throw' me. At the same time I must accept alterations made by the producer and incorporate them into my telling without altering the flow of the story. I may not agree with the alteration but I must accept it. Joy Whitby strongly objects to any 'softness' in a story and I must not use words like 'little' or 'tiny', as they are often sentimental. In a story I have been asked to write about a walk on a summer's day, details are removed which the presenters want to use themselves; I must omit these and add other details, all without faltering - quite difficult! I am asked to tell *The Little Red Engine*, including the noises and refrains and keeping up the pace, all this from memory. I tell a story of a river from its source to the sea. I must see it in my imagination – as a storyteller must – and, almost insensibly, my tone and pace reflect its flow; "beautifully told," says the producer.

These experiences are good training for all the storytelling I do. Discipline in the need to consider the value of every word helps me to realise the gift I have been trusted with all my life. "Your personality comes through more and more, and your sense of fun," says the producer. I feel encouraged. Storytelling is an essential part of my life.

My library children are much puzzled by my appearance on the screen, and their reaction is amusing.

A child rushes up to me in the post office. "I've seen you on telly!" she says, hugging me. Another little girl rushes to her mother in the kitchen, quite alarmed. "Miss Colwell has come into our house. How did she get here?" A boy accosts me in the library. "I saw you on telly! Next time will you say 'Hello David'! Then I shall really know you."

In 1965 I was asked to take part in a 'Jackanory' programme. This programme was aimed at children of five to nine years old and was planned to introduce stories of every kind – new and old, traditional and imaginative, published and new material. There was to be a daily programme on five days of the week.

I was asked to provide a miscellaneous programme first and, later, five days of stories by Eleanor Farjeon.

Recording these programmes for live television, was an exacting process. Each story occupied a whole morning. Work on the actual telling of the story was interrupted by breaks for voice tests, runthroughs of the script for the producer's alterations, technical checks, and make-up sessions for me from which I emerged outwardly glamorous and unfamiliar.

I was to sit on a platform in a most uncomfortable galvanised iron chair, beside a similar unattractive small table for my 'props'. I had to insist on a cushion in order to look relaxed. I knew my stories by heart but I was compelled to read them from an auto-cue which was propelled slowly by an old man who tried to adjust to my speed and dramatic pauses. I must have given him a hard time for I was used to the natural response of an audience. Also the whole narration was interspersed with snatches of filmed scenery and vocal effects, such as bird song, thought up by the producer. Occasionally there were mishaps, as when I was telling a story from Eleanor Farjeon's *Old Nurse's Stock-Basket*. I had to darn a large hole in the stage manager's sock with wool threaded by him. At the first stitch, the wool came out of the eye of the needle and I told the story darning assiduously in mime at intervals. Quite an ordeal!

No one who has experienced such moments, could ever forget the petrifying suspense as one waits for the whisper of the 'Jackanory' tune, followed by the knowledge that one must begin. Just before action, the floor manager crouches by my side and exhorts me to be calm, to smile and to imagine the million children who are going to love my story. The thought of so many children looking at me does not fill me with confidence. It terrifies me.

These appearances on the screen occupied five mornings for which I was paid £50 a morning. This seemed to me at the time an immense sum; I would have done the work for much less.

Another broadcast I remember, for its utter pointlessness, was at White City in the late 1960s. I am fetched by car for a ten o'clock item on 'Late Night Line Up', as the founder of Hendon's famous library. My chief memory is of bearded men with glasses in their hands, friendly enough but what is their function? My interviewer, who peers at me through a bush of hair, is completely disinterested in me, except for the trivial mention that I had once told stories in what had been a night-club in Miami Beach. Having elicited this odd bit of information, she relapses into her hair. The interview is over. What was it for?

I was fortunate to be involved in 'Jackanory' and 'Play School' in their formative stages and I learned much from this experience.

A programme televised in 1989, called 'By Word of Mouth', showed the importance of storytelling today, illustrating the significance of this traditional art to the ethnic races in Britain today and many sections of the community who find pleasure in it. I was asked to join one of the four programmes and this was recorded in my own home. I spoke about storytelling from my long experience and told stories in a school to a responsive group of children. The programmes were an indication of the resurgence of interest in storytelling in this country.

As I have said, in my own childhood radio and television were unknown, and I have watched their growth and development with interest and some apprehension as to their influence on social habits and on the lives of children in particular. It is indisputable that television has had an adverse effect on children's interest and involvement with books and reading. What does the future hold in this field as television grows more inventive in this computer age?

CHAPTER SEVENTEEN

In the period between the 1940s and 1960s, I was privileged to enjoy the friendship of two distinguished authors: John Masefield, the Poet Laureate, and the author and poet, Eleanor Farjeon.

My meeting with John Masefield came about in this way:

One morning in 1946, I found in my library post the following letter: "I wondered whether some day…you could permit me to be one of your listeners, if I promised to keep quiet?' It was signed 'John Masefield'. He had seen in the National Book League newsletter a photograph of me telling stories and thought I looked "awfully jolly".

I was soon to pay the first of my many visits to John Masefield at his home near Oxford. I knew him for twenty years, until his death in 1967.

On this, my first visit, I felt rather overawed. What would this distinguished man, author of so many plays, novels, children's books and – above all – poetry, be like? Would I find myself out of my depth? I need not have feared. When I arrived at Burcote Brook, Masefield was waiting at the door to welcome me. He was tall and spare with white hair and very blue eyes. He greeted me with an old world courtesy which was very welcome in our casual times.

Mrs Masefield, too, was welcoming, although a rather alarming lady, always wearing a hat in the house. She began asking me questions at once about books and children. Masefield alternated with remarks on storytelling. A visitor added her comments. "Tea!" said Mrs Masefield, and we trooped into another room.

"Now for a story!" We proceeded into the garden where we overlooked the shining river and golden harvest fields.

"Begin!" ordered Mrs Masefield and I stationed myself close to her ear, for she was very deaf. I began (with much trepidation) to tell them an amusing story which children loved. It was a success and the three adults laughed like children.

"Croquet, Jan!" said Mrs Masefield and we followed her obediently to the lawn. I had not played croquet since I was a child, but Masefield and I won – so he said, with a courtly bow.

My 'ordeal' was over, but it had not been an ordeal, for I had had such a friendly welcome, and such a warm invitation to come again that

I felt only pleasure as I was escorted to the bus and thanked for my 'gracious' visit.

This was to be the pattern of many visits. I grew accustomed to Constance Masefield's disconcerting way of switching me from a talk with John to one with her. It was not easy to converse with her, for she was so very deaf and one lens of her spectacles was much stronger than the other, so that I felt compelled to gaze into it. As time went by, we were to become good friends and she always made me welcome.

On one occasion, my sister and I took our marionettes and gave them a 'show'. It was delightful to see their pleasure in our puppets' antics.

After Mrs Masefield's death in 1960 – she was eleven years older than her husband – John Masefield and I continued to enjoy many times together. Jan would sit with his cat purring contentedly on his knees. Like Eleanor Farjeon, he loved cats.

His favourite had been Nibbins (who appears in *The Midnight Folk*), but in real life disappeared and was never found again, except in a reassuring dream.

Like Eleanor Farjeon also, Masefield had a limitless fund of stories which poured from his retentive memory, stories of magic and adventure, of romance and mystery. He delighted in finding tales of devils and demons and ghosts, particularly horrific tales of cannibals, to make my library children's 'blood run cold'. His eyes twinkled with fun as he watched my reaction. Some of these stories he found in Dickens' *Household Words*. One tale he told me, called *The Hopping Ha'penny*, he had heard from an Irishman he met in a remote part of Ireland. He 'gave' this to me to tell as it had never been written down and it was much loved by children, so I included it in one of my collections of stories. He spoke of his boyhood days on a sailing ship in the Mersey, a hard time. Long ago he met a man, a doctor, who had been Napoleon's surgeon. Another time, he talked to a lady whose cousin had seen Shelley when she was a child in the nursery. Asked what he would do with such naughty children, Shelley replied, "Give them oranges, Madam, and a tub of water to play in". Excellent advice!

Masefield once told me a true ghost story. A family he knew complained that they continually heard a child crying at the foot of the stairs of their cottage – the noise seemed to come from behind a panel. At last they could bear it no longer and got permission from the owners to remove the panel. Behind it were the bones if a young child. Its identity was never discovered, or the reason for its presence behind the panel. All records had been lost. So they buried the tiny skeleton and the cries were never heard again. (Jan had heard the cries himself.)

I told *him* stories, of course, for my experience and love of storytelling gave Masefield much pleasure. The oddest occasion, perhaps, was when I told him the story, at his request, of his own *Jim Davis*. He had quite forgotten this early book and when I finished he exclaimed, "I say, what a jolly good yarn!" I knew that his wife, had she been there, would have tried to stop this flow of conversation, for he had a heart condition and so much talk might not be good for him. But this was his life.

When I deputised for him at the first of the John Masefield Storytelling Festivals in Toronto in 1961, my subsequent report of my experiences gave him great pleasure. "Wot larks!" he said with his characteristic twinkle.

Although John Masefield had known hard times, an unhappy childhood and the grief of losing his only son in the Second World War, he enjoyed life. He was a generous and kindly man who had a gift for friendship and was deeply compassionate. I was always welcomed affectionately, a gift prepared for me, and even my birthday was remembered.

As the years went by I saw, with sorrow, his increasing frailty. With indifferent housekeepers and the weariness of age, life became difficult.

Still he wrote those characteristic single page letters to me about all kinds of things that interested him. He said, "We've been friends for so many years now and I do so enjoy it!"

Sadly the day came when he was taken ill and wrote his last letter to me, knowing, I am sure, that it was his last, for his daughter said he was very weary.

He had wished to have his ashes scattered in the countryside and he himself forgotten, for he was a humble man. His wishes were disregarded and he was honoured by being buried in Westminster Abbey, with 'pomp and circumstance'.

Although John Masefield left a wealth of poetry, plays and stories it was story*telling* that gave him the greatest joy. In his own words: "I have enjoyed stories, their making, telling and performing; and in all the happy process have been marvellously helped".

One afternoon in 1956 I walked down a cobbled lane in Hampstead to meet someone I had never met before in person, although I already knew her well through her books and stories. I knocked at the blue door which was to become so familiar and it was answered by a smiling old lady – Eleanor Farjeon. I had been asked by the American Library

Association to be the British representative in the storytelling programme at Miami Beach and I had come to ask her permission to tell my favourite story, and hers it transpired, *Elsie Piddock Skips in her Sleep*.

"Let me look at you," she said. "Yes, you are just as I hoped - you *are* Elsie Piddock!"

We make our way up the narrow staircase with a rope handrail, leading to the low-ceilinged room in which Eleanor Farjeon does her writing. Books spill from the shelves on to the floor and papers are heaped on the table. A low settee stands welcomingly before the fire and a basket chair sags comfortably beside it. Through the casement window, high in the eaves, we catch a glimpse, in their season, of blossoming fruit trees or bare wind-tossed branches and the backs of gracious old houses.

An imperious tap admits Benignus Malone, an imposing golden – not marmalade – cat, whose favourite resting-place is a bulging filing-box on the table beside his mistress. All cats love Eleanor Farjeon, and she them, and strays never lack for food and affection.

What a room this is, full of treasure of all kinds – books, music, a collection of lovely old fans, a tinkling music-box. It is a place of peace for the many people who visit here.

To hear one of the 'brilliant Farjeons' talking is an experience not to be forgotten. Spellbound, one listens while memories, anecdotes of people and places, experiences, pour forth effortlessly: children who skipped in the lane outside her Sussex cottage (Elsie Piddock amongst them); Robert Frost, who first showed Edward Thomas what poetry could be; magical islands off the coast of Brittany where she first dreamt of Martin Pippin; New York Public Library, where she was refused admission because there was a party and protested shyly, "But *I am* the party!" Stories, grave or hilariously funny, of meeting new friends, of receiving unexpected appreciation, are as absorbing to the listener as to her. "Such lovely things happen to me!" she says with pleasure. Indeed, it is this gift for the enjoyment of life and for seeing beauty and love in all around her, that shines through her poetry, from her poems for children, to her mature sonnets. Her fairytale plays are magical and haunting and her short stories (the most difficult of art forms) are wonderfully varied and skilful. Her collection of stories, *The Little Bookroom*, has won her three awards - the British Carnegie Medal, the international Hans Christian Andersen Medal and the American Regina Medal. These are received with characteristic astonishment and modesty.

Watch Eleanor as she talks. A plain old lady, you think? According to her own description to a too-persistent reporter over the telephone – she dislikes publicity – she has "gun-metal hair and a comfortable figure". But see her lively face with its curving smile and twinkling eyes behind her spectacles; here is someone whose eternally young spirit not even the accidents and cross-purposes of eighty years have succeeded in dimming.

"I'm beginning a new phase of life," she exclaims with anticipation, on recovering from an eye operation that would have prostrated younger people. Someone describes her as a 'frail old lady', and she laughs heartily at such a ridiculous idea. Self-pity is not for her, for everything that happens is valued as an opportunity for experience and joy. "It's so good to be alive, so interesting and so much fun!" Here is a person whose eyes and mind and heart are always wide open.

All are welcome in this room with its atmosphere of ease and harmony, and no one goes away but with a 'lift of the spirit'. "How kind everyone is!" says Eleanor Farjeon, but it is we who are the debtors for the loving kindness and wisdom of this rare person. We share in her inner happiness and serenity.

Bereft of so many of her generation and those loved companions of the *Nursery in the Nineties*, yet she makes new friends every day – "Friends have always come before anything else for me, even before my writing". Out of her wealth of love she gives and gives again, for she 'likes to be put upon'. Like Mrs Malone in her own poem, her heart is so big it has room for us all.

John Masefield and Eleanor Farjeon were of the same generation and members of the same literary circle. They had mutual friends – Walter de la Mare, for instance – and Masefield knew Herbert Farjeon, Eleanor's brother. Yet they never met!

It is intriguing to imagine a meeting. Both were poets, playwrights, writers of stories for adults and children. Both were fascinated by tradition and legends and classical times. Both, too, had an inexhaustible fund of stories and were born storytellers. Above all, they had a sense of fun and enjoyed life and found it intensely interesting. Each had faith in the eternal verities.

Looking back over forty years, I realise again how enriching these two friendships were. What a privilege it was to share, in however small a way, the affection of two such 'rare spirits'.

CHAPTER EIGHTEEN

I have been privileged to meet many interesting and notable people in my lifetime, mainly in the world of libraries and books. Such encounters with those, who not only have vision and lively minds, but also have achieved an aim in life and added to the well-being of the world around them, can only be of benefit. So it was with me. I was fortunate to meet a number of influential women, whose ideals and achievements inspired and stimulated me. All of them became my life-long friends. At this time, it was women rather than men who were predominant both in the library world and the children's book world. During my career in the 1930s and 1960s, I was to see the whole situation change. Women would become distinguished 'chiefs' and the children's books became 'big business'.

I have chosen to write about four women who influenced my life and development by their achievements and vision. It so happens that each came from a different country - England, America, Canada and Japan. And there is one other woman to whom I should like to pay tribute, for without her support at the very outset of my career in the development of the children's library service, I should not have met the women who are the subject of this chapter.

Alderman Mrs S.J. Bannister was the chairman of Hendon Libraries Committee. It was this gifted woman, the retired principal of a training college, who conceived the advertisement of the vacancy for a librarian to "create a library service, beginning with children", which was to fill me with hope for the future. It was Mrs Bannister who gave the casting vote which was to set me on the path to my ambition. I have often wondered what she saw in the young 'apple-cheeked girl' which persuaded her to select me from the six applicants. This was to be the passport to forty hard-working, happy years.

From the moment of my arrival at Hendon, Mrs Bannister gave me her support. She watched over my welfare, introduced me to the right people, found centres to act as temporary lending libraries, and supported me in any request I made to the council. We could talk about books and problems and plans for the children's department of the new library which was being built. This meant a great deal to me, for I had no one to advise me, as the chief librarian and the necessary staff were not appointed for two years. I could have had no better mentor, for she was wise and experienced in her contact with people of all kinds. She was kindly, but always had a dignity that impressed. I respected and admired her abilities and she was consistently appreciative of my ideas and efforts to make Hendon Children's Library system a truly good one. Her attitude to books and children was unusual at the time for, in those days (1926), children were only tolerated in a library. She was truly a 'pioneer'. It is salutary to realise that, had it not been for her support in those early days, I might never have realised my dream for a children's library.

As I have recounted, my first task when I took up my duties in Hendon was to build up a basic stock of children's books. I was determined that this should consist of not only the accepted 'classics' of children's literature, but also the best of modern books. On the advice of Mrs Bannister, I set out to visit the Bumpus Book Shop in Oxford Street. Now I was to have the exciting experience of actually *buying* books of my choice, a rather unnerving prospect at first, for I was now responsible for spending public money.

Mrs Bannister had not failed me. There could not have been a better place for my first assay in book-buying. In charge of the children's department was Mrs Bannister's friend, Eleanor Graham, and she too was building up a wide and personal knowledge of her stock by 'reading round the shelves' and so could really advise me from her own knowledge. We were to become firm friends until her death.

Eleanor Graham was to become the Children's Book Editor with Heinemann and Methuen. For a time she worked as librarian at a private library, in order to observe children's reactions to specific books. Finally, she made the most important move of her life to Penguin Books, for here it was that she founded the famous Puffin Books for children in 1941 - a paperback series, unheard of at that time. A very important innovation, this was the first paperback series published for children in which quality of imagination and writing were the criteria. Eleanor Graham chose modern books – not the 'classics' of children's literature – which had proved their worth; for example, *The Family From One End Street* by Eve Garnett and *Worzel Gummidge* by Barbara Euphan Todd. Later, she commissioned books for the series, and my own anthologies of stories and poetry for young children were among these.

All her choices had to satisfy her standards but also to appeal to children. From the beginning, the series established an excellence and a standard that had not been seen before. Every new addition must pass her critical judgement of style and imagination. The Puffins are still best sellers, but subsequent editors have not always been as selective.

During the years that followed, Eleanor Graham became well known in the children's book world as critic, editor, and as a writer herself. She was the first to win recognition for children's books as worthy subjects for review and wrote regularly in such established journals as the *Sunday Times* and the *Bookman*. Later, her thoughtful reviews were to be important in establishing the only periodical for the regular reviewing of books for children, the *Junior Bookshelf*.

As a writer, she maintained her own high standards, producing excellent anthologies of verse and her deeply-felt *Life of Jesus*. One of her stories, *The Children Who Lived in a Barn*, was a 'blue print' for the modern stories of self-reliant boys and girls, sensible but adventurous.

She was very much a pioneer in establishing the right of children's books to be considered as 'literature', requiring standards of production and writing as stringent as those for adults.

Eleanor Graham's influence on me was considerable, I realise. We met often, privately and at public functions and on literary committees. We had an easy relationship and I was at home in her flat at the top of an old house in Soho. Her brother - Stephen Graham, the traveller - lived in the same building and I knew his absorbing books on his adventures. It was always stimulating, but strangely restful, to spend an evening with Eleanor Graham. I hope her innate wisdom and attitude to life made me a little wiser and more tolerant in my turn. Her standards in literature for children were much my own and she would not allow any weakening, whatever the temptation, although this did not mean she lacked a sense of humour.

She won the Eleanor Farjeon Award in 1973, for her contribution to the cause of children's literature. Modest, unassuming, a woman of integrity, warmth and humour, Eleanor Graham was a pioneer in many avenues of children's literature what she made her particular concern.

I first met Virginia Haviland in 1955, when we were both involved with our European colleagues in the formation of the Children's Libraries Committee of the International Federation of Library Associations. Virginia was to have a considerable influence on my life and career, for it was through her contacts that I was invited to go to the United States for the first time. We attended the same international conferences and we took the opportunity to extend our journeys and to visit new countries together. In her company, my horizons were widened, my professional knowledge of books and libraries increased, and my life enriched through her friendship. Every year, she stayed in our home and we exchanged news and opinions on professional matters. This contact was both valuable and pleasant. At the time (the 1950s), Virginia was Readers' Advisor for Children in Boston Public Libraries. She was already an experienced librarian with an exceptionally wide knowledge of children's literature, and her critical mind had established her as a welcome reviewer. With these abilities and qualifications, it was not surprising that, in 1963, she was approached by the Library of Congress to undertake the organisation of the extensive resources in children's books and related material that existed there.

This was an apt appointment, for Virginia proved to be an expert administrator and used the valuable material at hand to advantage in the production of bibliographical tools, reading lists and catalogues of the exhibitions she planned with such imagination. The Centre rapidly became a rich source of information for students. The Library of Congress's annual celebrations for the National Children's Book Week which she instituted, addressed by prestigious authors and illustrators from many countries, were outstanding festive occasions.

Virginia Haviland was an inveterate traveller, 'an international grasshopper', attending innumerable conferences and serving as chairman of many committees, notably the Hans Christian Andersen jury and its parent body, where her influence was especially significant. She enjoyed these conferences and I watched with awe as she concentrated her gaze on the speaker whilst, at the same time, making copious notes. She rightly disapproved of my desire to play truant from boring meetings and she took it as my duty to be there. I responded by luring her away for very necessary relaxation. On these international journeys her first concern was to secure examples of the country's best books for children, for she became an official ambassador for her library.

In her own country she was an esteemed authority on children's literature, serving as adjudicator, critic and lecturer, with indefatigable energy. Her work was honoured by the Regina Medal and the Grolier Foundation Award.

Her true and lasting memorial, however, is the Centre she served so wholeheartedly. It is the visible proof of her abiding faith in the value of books in the lives of children and the assured place of children's books in the main stream of literature.

Her energy was formidable and her achievements outstanding.

Virginia Haviland was truly a pioneer in the world of books for children. Nevertheless, she was no cold career woman. I knew her as a gracious and generous person and dear friend.

Lillian H. Smith was born in Ontario, Canada in 1887. Her father was a Methodist minister. As a child she read widely, for the love of books, which were to play a large part in her life, was already evident.

In 1910, at the age of twenty-three, she enrolled in the Training School of Children's Librarians at Pittsburgh in America. It was there that the opportunity which was to shape her life came her way. Anne Carroll Moore of New York Public Library's 'Children's Room', asked Pittsburgh to send her an 'outstanding student to establish a service to children in Toronto'. Lillian Smith was chosen and, after an exacting year of training with Anne Carroll Moore, she travelled to Toronto in 1912 to begin what was to be her life's work.

With her critical ability and her knowledge of books for children already considerable, she chose the stock of her library. From the beginning, she instituted a programme of storytelling and those activities for which she had room. In 1922 she secured the house which was to be Boys and Girls House, the only library of its kind, and with a *trained* children's librarian, in the British Empire. Although the United States had a progressive system for children, England had little provision for them and, in fact, offered almost no encouragement to children to use a library at all.

Now Lillian Smith *could* extend her service. All kinds of imaginative activities took shape and Boys and Girls House became an exciting place and a haven for the children of Toronto. The basis of everything, however, was the extensive stock of carefully chosen books, representing all tastes and the very best literature available for boys and girls. Lillian Smith's knowledge of literature and her informed critical sense were evident in everything. She had gathered a band of librarians round her who, however different their personalities, supported her plans for service to the children of Toronto.

In 1927, she edited her catalogue *Books for Boys and Girls*, which was recognised as a standard source of reference for librarians.

Boys and Girls House, now sadly closed, became a Mecca for library students and others from all parts of the world, some of whom were privileged to work there for a time to gain experience of this unique library for children. Her influence within her profession was considerable for, in 1939, she founded the Association of Canadian

Children's Librarians, the forerunner of the Canadian Library Association.

In 1953, Lillian Smith wrote *The Unreluctant Years*, in which she not only discussed the various categories of children's literature such as Fairy Stories, Poetry and Historical Fiction, but also expressed her convictions and philosophy on choosing books for children and her abiding belief that "only the best is good enough for children".

She received many tributes for her service to books and children, but surely the greatest and most valuable gift made in her honour was that of the Osborne Collection of Early Children's Books. Edgar Osborne – an English librarian – had offered this valuable collection to England, but no institution had the funds essential for its care. Toronto accepted it and eventually made provision for a fund for additions and appointed a trained librarian, Judith St John. This collection is the largest and most comprehensive in the world. It was solely due to Lillian H. Smith's outstanding achievement that it found its home in Toronto. Later, the Osborne Collection was supplemented by books from the Lillian Smith Collection.

I met Lillian Smith after her retirement in 1956, when I made my first visit to Canada. I felt I already knew her, for I had read *The Unreluctant Years*, in which she shared so much of her beliefs and guiding principles - so very like those of Eleanor Graham. We had much in common in our background, and each had had encounters with prejudice and bureaucracy. We felt at ease immediately and became friends. I appreciated her forcefulness and her ironic humour, for here was someone whose wisdom and achievement I respected and admired.

Lillian H. Smith died in 1983, her interest in children and books still strong to the last. Her own words, written for me in her book, could well be her epitaph: "The mind knows only what dwells near the heart".

The greatest influence on the development of children's literature in Japan this century has been that of Momoko Ishii. Editor, author, translator and critic, this has always been her interest.

Momoko Ishii was born in 1907 in Urawa-shi, Saitama-ken in Japan. She came from a family of nine brothers and sisters, so knew something of children and their differences.

Momoko Ishii was educated at the Japanese University for Women, specialising in the study of English Literature and the English Language, a foundation which was to serve her well. On graduating in 1928, she made an important decision, for she took a post with a leading publisher, becoming familiar with the problems of editing and publishing. This was all useful training. Now Miss Ishii set out to investigate what books for children were available in Japan. She joined a well known author of the time in the compilation of a booklist for boys.

In 1937 she read a copy of *Winnie the Pooh* by A. A. Milne. This was a new experience for her, for there was nothing as whimsical as this in Japanese literature for children. Would they appreciate such a blend of humour and fantasy?

She began the translation of English and American children's 'classics' which was to open a new world of enjoyment to Japanese children. Today visitors will recognise many favourites on Japanese library shelves. Perhaps no one but a translator can realise the problems of translation from one language to another, especially in books as idiosyncratic as those of A.A. Milne, Tolkien, and Kenneth Grahame, for instance.

During World War Two, and its aftermath of American occupation, a period of disaster and suffering for the Japanese, Momoko Ishii left Tokyo and lived on a farm in Miyagi. Perhaps this period of country life helped to build up her energies again, for she came back to Tokyo in 1951 to continue her work in the field of children's literature, editing two series of books, one for girls, the other for boys. Then came her breakthrough. Her early children's book – *Non-chan Rides the Clouds*, originally published in 1947 - was recognised by the Minister for Education and was eventually republished, becoming a great success. The money she earned in this way she gave to help farmers in the provinces (who had been hard hit by the War).

In 1953, she won the Kikuchi Kan Award for her contribution to children's literature. These successes secured her a Rockefeller Scholarship for a year's study of children's literature and libraries in the USA and the UK, an experience of which she took full advantage. On her return to Japan, she retired from her editorial work in order to study, as far as possible, the actual relationship between books and children. How did they respond to the books we chose so arbitrarily for them?

In order to observe children more closely, she worked with them in a small village in north-east Japan, then by setting up a 'bunko' in her own home – 'Katsura Bunko'.[1]

From this time on, Momoko Ishii was active in forming groups of interested people to discuss and study children's books and libraries. These groups instigated experiments in connections with books and

---

[1] *For more about the 'bunko movement' see Chapter Twenty Two*

children, with varying success. The result was a book in 1960 about their experiences, entitled *Children and Literature*, which proved a sensation, for its conclusions transformed the traditional idea about books for children.

Later, this same group attracted particularly imaginative, enterprising members, three of whom - Kyoko Matsuoka, Riyoko Sasa and Tokuko Arai - founded Tokyo Children's Library, to which I gave my collection of books on children's libraries and literature, when I retired in 1967.

In 1961, Momoko Ishii visited Europe and the United States of America and attended a storytelling festival in Toronto. This visit confirmed her belief that libraries were essential for the encouragement and creation of the best books for children. It was a pleasure to meet Momoko again (this was the year I went to Toronto as John Masefield's envoy) – our last meeting had been at my home in London. I had many engagements at the Festival, but Momoko and I were able to visit Lillian Smith at her country home, The Sheiling.

In 1965, after seven years working with children and books in her own bunko, she wrote of her experiences in *Children's Library*, a most valuable record of the meetings between books and boys and girls. This book was read widely and included an account of her visits abroad and inspired many new bunkos all over Japan.

As it happen, our next meeting was also in Toronto, in 1967, where we were both delegates at the Conference of the International Federation of Library Associations. Again we drove out to The Sheiling. Lillian Smith, now eighty, welcomed us with her sweet smile. Her friends had given her a somewhat unusual gift - a lake near her home! Momoko and I embarked on a small, leaking boat, our feet in water. Small green frogs stared at us, bulbous-eyed, amongst the water-lilies. There was a sound of falling water and the sun was hot as we sculled in circles – it was all great fun! Lillian Smith watched us benevolently from the bank. It is a treasured memory, for here were three women from three continents, renewing a friendship based on a mutual concern for books and children the world over.

In 1972, Momoko Ishii – with her usual thoroughness – visited England specifically for the purpose of making herself familiar with the backgrounds of Beatrix Potter and Eleanor Farjeon. Eleanor Farjeon's country home in Sussex and the 'House with the Blue Door' in Hampstead, gave her great pleasure, as did Beatrix Potter's cottage in Lakeland. She had translated many of Beatrix Potter's well known books and now they were almost as familiar to Japanese as to English children. Momoko Ishii has always been a skilled translator, particularly of English literature for children, sensing the very nuances of the language.

She has never lost her interest in libraries for children and in 1977 she became a member of the board of Tokyo Children's Library. Japan is proud, and rightly so, of Momoko Ishii's record in the growth of a distinctive Japanese literature for children and a library service, not only in public libraries, but in the unique and distinctive bunko service in private homes.

It is fitting that she should have been awarded the Yomiuri Prize (1995) for her own autobiographical novel, *Maboroshi No Akai Mi*, when she was eighty-nine. I know the book cost her much to complete, for it was written from the heart.

I have tried to convey something of Momoko Ishii's achievements as writer, editor and translator. Her influence in Japanese children's literature and the library provision for children has been decisive, and her name will long be remembered. I am honoured to have been her friend for so many years and to have shared her beliefs and ideals.

Pioneers are essential for every new cause, great or small. Someone with vision and determination must take the first step.

The five women I have chosen were all deeply concerned for standards in children's literature and for the right of boys and girls to have access to books, whatever their station in life or their nationality. Even if the next generation forgets them, their influence for their common cause remains a firm foundation on which others can build.

PART SIX

TO SEE THE QUEEN;
SECOND RETIREMENT

CHAPTER NINETEEN

In 1965, to my great surprise, I was awarded the MBE, the 'Grant of the Dignity of an Ordinary Member of the Civil Division of the Order of the British Empire', for my services to children's books and libraries. This is an award which might be called the 'People's Medal', for it can be – and is – awarded to any individual who has contributed service for the common good, from traffic warden to high ranking local official. I valued this award particularly because it was the first time that the importance and value of books and library services to children had been recognised publicly.

The award came in the preliminary form of a letter from Buckingham Palace to ask whether I would be willing to accept such an award if I were asked. I certainly would! But I had to wait to tell anyone until the Honours List appeared. On that date, I hastened to break the news to my landlady, the only person available. "I've been awarded the MBE!" I told her. "Isn't it exciting!" "A lot of people in Hendon have the MBE," remarked Miss B laconically. So much for fame! I set off for the library deflated.

I found to my surprise that my 'Chief' knew all about it as he had been consulted months ago. The Red Letter Day arrived when I went to Buckingham Palace to 'see the Queen' like the cat in the nursery rhyme. My sister and sister-in-law went with me in an elegant hired car which the taxi driver had been polishing since early in the morning. We were elegant in new clothes. As we drove, I reflected how ironical is was that the Order of the Most Excellent Order of the British Empire should be awarded at a time when the Empire had virtually disappeared and we were engaged in giving away any odd bits that remained.

We drove up the Mall in grand style at a funeral pace, as we were part of a long queue. The sky was grey and the trees leafless on that February day. At the palace gates we were checked before we moved into the forecourt, past the sentries in their grey coats and busbies, to the main entrance where my companions had to leave me. Red carpets were everywhere for the privileged and we gathered in a gallery where we were checked again and a hook was put in the lapel of our coats,. This was for the Queen to hang the medal on – how sensible. Imagine having to pin 150 medals in 150 coats.

I looked round at my fellow medallists; men from the forces, civil servants, mostly elderly. One old man looked in imminent danger of falling on to his nose and was held up by an equerry. But where were the women? This was the first medal to be awarded to women as well as men at the wish of Queen Mary, so that women also might be honoured after World War One. I estimated that there were not more than twenty women that day amongst the 150. So much for the equality of women. However, next to me there was a women in a smart military uniform. She told me that she had 'thumbed' a lift from Singapore with the RAF. She was a major in rank and had served in the Far East Command for ten years. Only one other woman looked as smart as the major. Most of us were wearing our winter coats with new hats and gloves and shoes. There were three young people amongst our elderly crowd, olympic medallists, whose portraits I had seen in the newspaper.

I couldn't but be aware of the man in front of me, for he was a six-foot Yeoman of the Guard with the Royal Arms in heavy gold embroidery on his back.

We were rehearsed in the procedure. The Queen would be on a dais, we were to walk forward, curtsey, take three steps forward and shake her hand - *when* she offered it. Three steps backward, curtsey again, and walk away. No chattering or giving her our life histories (do people really attempt this?). The equerry demonstrated the bow for the men. "What about our curtsey?" asked a woman's voice, but such frivolity was out of place here.

A contingent was formed up and marched off at the double. The service-women went first, led by our female major. We followed in single file behind an equerry. I could see nothing ahead of me as the Yeoman was immediately in front.

We walked past galleries and windows curtained in rose pink and gilt. There were paintings on the walls, some of which I recognised. There were also mirrors in which I saw myself reflected far too often.

In the great ballroom in which the investiture was to be held, there were tiers of seats – my family was somewhere there, but I could not look for we were marshalled forwards. Surely someone should have been shouting "Left! Right!" Soft romantic music was being played and, somewhere ahead of me, the Queen was waiting.

Stanley Matthews had already been made a Knight at an earlier ceremony. A modern knight in his tail coat, his only weapon a football, he had knelt before the Queen for his accolade. The Dames and Commanders (CBE) and Officers of the Order (OBE) had already been 'processed'. Then we common MBEs were to have our turn.

We females practised our curtsey, watched tolerantly by the equerries who were in charge of us. Our names were checked once more in case they had changed. We caught a glimpse of the Queen. Yeoman of the Guard were behind her and she was flanked by two officials – one held a black velvet cushion on which the medals were set out. The other read out names as we appeared.

Alas, the Queen was not wearing her crown – the children at the library were disappointed to hear that. She was a light, youthful figure, in a simple apricot-coloured day dress. She wore little jewellery. She was laughing and animated.

Then it was my turn. An official checked my name for the third time, in case I had changed it at the last moment, and read out: "EILEEN_COLWELL"...I moved forward smartly, curtsied, walked three steps forwards (all safe so far). I had time to notice that the Queen was even more attractive close to and she did *not* appear heavily made up. She hung the medal on the hook on my coat, and asked pleasantly what I did. I answered, and she commented "That sounds interesting!" I said "It is!" and she shook my hand. I stepped three steps backward, curtsied (without falling), and walked away. For one short moment in my life – my "lovely moment," as Eleanor Farjeon called it - the Queen's attention had been focused on me. A not-to-be-forgotten moment, for it was the recognition of years of service. I was glad my family could share in it, and that my brother Eric knew of it before he died.

Outside, I found Vera and Una, and we moved into the courtyard. The other medallists moved across the stage, each with her 'moment' she or he would never forget. Our car arrived and we drove home to a reception from our neighbours. We drank sherry – "Nasty stuff!" said Miss B and left most of it.

There were cables of congratulation from Boys and Girls House in Toronto, from Virginia in Washington, from the Secretary of State for Education and Science, from publishers, librarians, booksellers. I received 80 letters from many parts of the world. An article about me appeared in India (but nothing in Hendon). Parents and children congratulated me. A little girl of four hugged me; other small children asked me about the Queen's crown (Oh, why didn't she wear it!). A Russian Jew compelled his child of two – who had a feeding bottle hanging out of her mouth – to take my hand and throw a kiss to me. Children drew pictures of the ceremony, with me hand-in-hand with the Queen and chatting cosily over a cup of tea. She was, of course, wearing her crown.

All this was warming; but best of all was to know what I was the first children's librarian to receive this honour and that, in my person, all children's librarians were being recognised: a public acknowledgement of the value of books and libraries for children, once the Cinderella of the profession.

CHAPTER TWENTY

One sunny day in August 1967 I left Hendon, where I had lived for forty years, to begin a new life in the Midlands town of Loughborough in Leicestershire. My sister Vera and I planned to make a home together, for I had been appointed as a lecturer in the University of Loughborough. She, too, was leaving her cottage in Lutterworth to join me. It was a new life for both of us and we looked forward to it.

We knew nothing of Loughborough, but both liked the idea of living in the country, and we were delighted to find fields and woods and country walks almost on our doorstep, for Loughborough is surrounded by vestiges of the ancient forest of Charnwood and boasts the most lofty hill – the Beacon - in the flat countryside of Leicestershire.

In 1965, Hendon had became part of the Borough of Barnet, the second largest borough in London. I had been promoted to be Librarian-in-Charge of the children's and school libraries of the new borough and asked to stay on - I was now sixty-one - long enough to amalgamate and establish the system. This was no mean task, for it comprised twenty junior and 150 school libraries. It was sad for me to leave my library and remove to new headquarters in Finchley. It also meant losing my daily contact with children, amongst whom I have made so many friends. No added status and new challenges could make up for this.

My years in my new position were intensely busy, but it would be tedious to itemise them. Obviously my work was to ensure that the system for children was a comprehensive one. In order to secure this, I visited all my library centres, both in libraries and schools, so that I would be aware of what was needed to maintain a good service. I had also established a good relationship with those in charge. Occasional conferences on books and library matters were appreciated and my branch librarians came to a monthly meeting where we discussed which books to buy for their individual libraries.

Now I had been asked to be Assistant Lecturer in the Department of Librarianship in the university, under the direction of Phyllis Parrott, my friend and colleague of many years, who had founded the section for Library Work with Children. I decided to accept, as I was contemplating retirement. My post in Hendon was increasingly busy but was well established and my work had, of necessity, become administrative in the main. I like to be involved with people, preferably children. I still regretted severance from 'my library' at Hendon, so I announced my retirement.

It was a sad time for me, for I visited everyone, especially the local primary school with which I had a special relationship from the beginning. All the 300 children were gathered together to say goodbye. Every child, however young, had signed their name and they sang to me and gave me flowers and, most treasured of all, their affection. This was what made my work all worthwhile and I was grateful.

My chief assistant in the Junior Library had already presented me with a wonderful retirement present, a book in which everyone in the library service, from Chief Librarian to caretakers and 'Mrs Mops,' was represented. Most valued of all, the children who used the library, many of them my Junior Library Helpers, had written their names and messages. Teachers, too, were there. To this day, over thirty years after, it gives me pleasure and I remember again those who showed me this affection.

The final ceremony of my retirement had to come. I was to receive the customary present (a gold watch) and listen to the final speeches. But here there was an unexpected quirk of humour, for my watch was presented by an elderly alderman who had been a member of the committee which selected me forty years ago and – what is more – he referred to me as "the apple-cheeked young woman" whom he helped to choose. My staff looked at me in amazement – could this elderly lady really have been young and 'apple-cheeked'? In that moment, I was that young woman again with her dream which had been so wonderfully realised. How blessed I was.

Before I took up my new duties at the university, I had to attend the IFLA Conference to represent England on the Committee on Library Work with Children. The conference was to be in Toronto – now quite familiar to me – and included a tour through Canada to Quebec. It was an opportunity to meet old friends and to make new ones, a pleasant occasion.

Looking back, I realise that I might have found it difficult to accept a subservient post after I had been my own mistress for so long. Fortunately this did not occur to me for, after all, I had much to learn and knew little of the life of a university and – most importantly – of modern students. I was an experienced lecturer, but most of my engagements seldom comprised more than one or two lectures, and I planned their contents myself. Now I must keep to a syllabus – sometimes on aspects of librarianship of which I knew little – and I must repeat lectures year after year. I must be sure of dates and information for these exam-ridden students, and I must not be too frivolous. In all my work, my 'chief' could not have been more helpful, but my tendency to be informal must have been a trial to her at times, for she was a very capable lecturer, with a great concern for her students and their welfare.

I often found individual students a problem, for some had chosen the subject of library work with children as an 'easy option' – which it was not, for it required much specialist knowledge and an understanding of children. Some students regarded university life as a period for social pleasures and so developed 'problems', with which I was not always in sympathy.

After two years, I realised that I did not want to continue this 'hard labour'. I preferred to have a less regimented life and to regain contact with children and storytelling; to be myself. I realised, too, my limitations in this kind of lecturing.

In 1968, Roy Stokes, Director of the Department of Library Studies, suggested holding an international summer conference at Loughborough University on Literature for Children. He thought now that Phyllis Parrott had an assistant, this might be possible.

It was a big undertaking, for we had not only the programme to arrange, but also all the accommodation for the students. The university would make a grant towards expenses for guest speakers. Here my knowledge proved useful, for I could contact suitable people on a personal basis, and ask for their co-operation. The conference was not intended to be a regular event, but, as it happened, it was arranged and hosted by a different country each year until 1984, and was a welcome occasion for an interchange of ideas and experiences. The countries included Holland, Germany, Denmark and even the USA. Each conference ended with a storytelling session. Having served its purpose, the final school was held in Australia in 1984.

For ten years or so after my retirement from Loughborough University, I travelled up and down Britain, lecturing and telling stories. I had no lack of engagements, for I was known in the world of education and librarianship. This was a happy and relaxed time for me, because I no longer had the stress of the heavy responsibility for a large

159

library system for children, or that of students at the university. I could choose my engagements and their location, and their themes were those which were the main interest of my life – books and storytelling. I had always enjoyed meeting people, particularly children; now I was able to concentrate on these pleasures. Above all, these activities provided a stimulus for me, very necessary when one is approaching one's eighties.

I was fortunate in that Vera was now living with me in our new home, so that I had someone to welcome me when I returned from my journeys, someone who enjoyed hearing about my 'adventures', and even sharing them when the venue was attractive, or when I needed a 'co-driver' on my country journeys. Otherwise, Vera was happy with her garden and church activities and her music pupils.

My travels took me the length and breadth of the British Isles: from Kirkcaldy in Scotland to Taunton in Somerset; from Cardiff to Skegness. I visited cities and villages, spoke to playgroups and Women's Institutes, to universities and libraries. Audiences ranged from pre-school children to grandmothers. Above all, I told stories to at least ten thousand children. And, of course, I had the pleasure of seeing unfamiliar and beautiful parts of Britain. I was talking all the time about libraries and every aspect of books and, above all, telling stories.

My journeys were full of interest because of the people I met, of all ages and and from all parts of society. My audiences were very varied. On one occasion I numbered seventeen of Her Majesty's Inspectors, who listened as attentively as any children. The size of an audience was of little importance in storytelling, for 400 children could be a spellbound by a good story as half a dozen. Also, boys and girls appreciated the sound of words. "Oh, them lovely words!" exclaimed a girl after hearing a Greek legend; and another child said, "Words jump out at you".

Storytime with the youngest children was a delight. I had, as my only 'prop', a glove puppet (given to me in Japan) with a red cloth body and a pleasant cheeky face. 'Jacko' was a comfort to many timid little children and set them at ease. He was completely real to the children, so I conducted conversations with him. I told them he wanted a banana. Imaginary bananas were almost always available. On one occasion, I disposed of the (imaginary) skin on the chair behind me. As I sat down at the end of the story, one hundred children shouted simultaneously "Miss! You've sat on the banana skin!" I jumped up as if I had been shot!

My adult audiences were often challenging with their questions. There was always one on the controversial subject of Enid Blyton, and I enjoyed the 'give and take' of opinion and knowledge.

CHAPTER TWENTY-ONE

These years of my second retirement were happy ones, for not only was I still active but I also received public recognition for my work for children and books in the library world.

An award came to me in 1974 from an unexpected source: Manchester Polytechnic. It is the custom of these large polytechnics (now universities) to honour men and women who have made a significant contribution to public causes for the good of society. On this occasion, I was extraordinarily fortunate in the two other recipients who were honoured at the same time. They were Jack Ashley, the Member of Parliament, and Yehudi Menuhin, the famous musician. Jack Ashley had become totally deaf, but had overcome his disability with great courage and kept his seat in Parliament.

It was a privilege to walk between these two noted and pleasant men, to take my seat beside them. As we walked up to the platform, we were instructed to "Start off with your left foot" by the chief usher. We did our best. I was immediately behind Jack Ashley (who is tall) and behind me was Yehudi Menuhin, relaxed and smiling. "I feel like the filling in the sandwich," I said to Yehudi. "The most delicious jam!" he said gallantly.

The tribute to one's achievements on these occasions always leave me wondering – like the old woman in the nursery rhyme – "Is this really me?" At the dinner that evening, Yehudi Menuhin gave one of his famous speeches, a medley of idealism and philosophy, which was too long for such an occasion and left everyone dazed but uplifted.

In 1975, Loughborough University made me a Doctor of Literature, a tribute once again to the importance of children and books. This academic recognition gave me a particular pleasure – nothing would have given me more satisfaction than to have earned this by study.

The occasion, with its traditional formality – and caps, gowns and solemnity - was impressive, but had a touch of comicality. I must have looked particularly small against the three six-foot men in their scarlet robes who were receiving Doctorates at the same time. Added to this, my black, stiff mortar-board proved to be too large for my small head, and only my ears held it in place. As I stood on the platform for my official 'Oration' and the ribbon was placed over my head, my 'cap' eclipsed me! There was no sound, as the audience of several hundred students dozed in the hot afternoon. I wished I was allowed to laugh!

In 1994, when I was ninety, I was honoured by the presentation of the Eleanor Farjeon Award, instituted by the publishers of children's books. To receive such a prize, when I was no longer part of the world of children's books, was a particular pleasure. My good friend Helen Cresswell, author of many books for children, was my supporter and invaluable friend, on this occasion as always, for I had to travel to London for the presentation. It was pleasant to meet old friends from the book world, but I realised that probably I was the only person there who had actually known Eleanor Farjeon as a living person. To them she was a name on a title-page. To me she was a warm, gifted woman, a poet and teller of stories - especially the one she had 'given' to me as her favourite, *Elsie Piddock Skips in her Sleep*.

All my life has been bound up with my storytelling. Now, in old age, I was to know – and take a small part in – a revival of the art of storytelling, not particularly amongst librarians, but a movement from the heart of the people. In 1993 the Society for Storytelling was founded and at the inaugural meeting, Philippa Pearce read a tribute to me written by Marcus Crouch. To be so closely associated with this budding movement by two such friends was a great pleasure. The Society is now officially established and the art of storytelling is enthusiastically practised in an intriguing variety of forms and backgrounds.

CHAPTER TWENTY-TWO

In 1976 I was invited to visit Japan. I owe this privilege to two people in particular, Kyoko Matsuoka, Director of the Tokyo Children's Library, translator and author, and Momoko Ishii. My visit was sponsored, very generously, from a fund set up by C. Itoh Co. Ltd., one of the major export-import companies of Japan. The following account of my visit is based on my own observations. Any errors of fact or understanding are mine alone.

Momoko had already written of my storytelling in her book on the home libraries, hence my name was not unknown in Japan and I had friends there who had visited me in England. My invitation was to deliver public lectures and to take part in a seminar on work with children and children's literature.

"What is this 'lecturing'?" asked the passport official on my arrival in Tokyo. "I am going to talk about children's literature," I replied. "What are you going to say?" he asked, preparing to listen while the queue waited. What indeed!...I moved on hastily.

Tokyo, a vast city, was overwhelming and, for a visitor, complicated by the fact that there are no names on the streets and the numbers of the houses are not in strict numerical order. Fortunately, I was always accompanied by a Japanese librarian and so had no problem finding my way or calculating Japanese currency.

One of my first engagements was a reception in my honour, attended by an impressive array of officials representing such bodies as the Japanese Library Association, the British Council, UNESCO, education authorities, publishers and other organisations connected with children and books. I was delighted to meet a past member of a storytelling group I led at the Froebel Institute. She was now teaching the Imperial children using the technique I had taught her for telling stories. Here, too, I met Mrs Shiego Tsuchiya, the original instigator of home libraries, an activity in which I was particularly interested. Everyone was welcoming and we all bowed and smiled exhaustingly.

One of my first visits was to Momoko Ishii's home library. She had extended her family home to accommodate it. It was a busy, happy place with many children from the neighbourhood borrowing books or listening to a story (*Epaminondas* that day!). The whole history of the home libraries is of considerable significance for children and books.

home libraries, called 'bunku', which means 'treasure house of literature', became influential in the 1960s and 1970s due to the enthusiasm of Momoko Ishii and her friends at a time when Japan was recovering from the devastation of the Second World War. More attention was being paid to children and their welfare, and women had more leisure and interest in community affairs.

Katei bunku are small informal libraries with an intimate atmosphere, situated mostly in private homes and consisting of the family's books supplemented by gifts and, sometimes, a small subscription from the borrowers. They are usually open one day a week and run by volunteers - the housewife and her friends. In 1984, a survey, headed by Professor Satoru Takeuchi, showed that there were between four and five thousand bunku – many times the number of public libraries providing a service for children – to be found in Japan. When I last researched the matter, Tokyo alone had 221 and every prefecture has some at least. The 15,000 volunteers involved are mainly housewives – very few men take part – half are in private homes, 20% in co-operative housing or community halls. The movement has spread also to Christian churches and Buddhist temples which provide books for their child members.

From the bunku movement, a remarkable service has developed which has had considerable influence on the service offered by public libraries and bunku. In the 1970s, bunku in Japan formed themselves into associations. In Tokyo, the four largest bunku united to form what is now called the Tokyo Children's Library. The prime movers in this change were Momoko Ishii and Kyoko Matsuoka (who had her home rebuilt in order to provide better premises for the library). Kyoko had been trained as a librarian, hoping to be able to train and encourage librarians working with children from *within* the library service. She found that bureaucracy hampered all initiative, so she returned to the freedom to be found in the bunku movement outside the 'establishment'. Tokyo Children's Library now provides an extensive and varied service to those who work in libraries of any kind, whether public or private. The library's journal *Kodomo Tosho Kan* carries reviews, articles on relevant topics and booklists. Over three hundred storytellers have been trained and now give pleasure in libraries and hospitals.

Lectures and workshops are arranged as, for instance, those in which I took part. When I visited the Tokyo Children's Library, local women were attending a course in storytelling and obviously enjoying it. There is now a course on book reviewing and the writing of annotations as well as instruction in children's literature. In 1976, a 'model' central Children's Room was opened.

I visited the headquarters which also served as a library, small but attractive. The eight members of staff with their director, Kyoko, organise courses and compile booklists, and discuss books, creating a centre from which spring new ideas and enthusiasms.

The public library system of Japan has been slow to develop, partly because the Japanese, where books are concerned, are more naturally a *buying* public than a borrowing one. Most library provision is in the cities; only 14% in rural areas or small towns. Provision is made for children but it is unequal and inadequate. Surely, as more young people are trained in America and the West, the modern conception of libraries should gain ground and the attitude of authorities change?

There is little training for library work and none for work with children. It is obvious, therefore, how valuable is the work done in this field by Tokyo Children's Library, both in practical instruction and, equally important, encouragement. Children's librarians have no status as such and are hampered by a strange system of local government which provides no 'job security'. Any assistant working for a local authority can be transferred arbitrarily from one department to another. One librarian told me with bitterness that she was taken from the work she loved in the children's department for four years before she was allowed to return. Another, who had no aptitude for working with children, was put in the junior library where she was an unhappy misfit. At another library, a woman was appointed to be charge over other more experienced assistants because she had a child and therefore knew 'all about children'. Such a system provides no incentive to work for qualifications and stifles enthusiasm.

There is only one library school in Tokyo, provided by American influence, but there the emphasis is on computer science rather than service in a public library. The graduates, finding that they can obtain better salaries in industry as information officers, choose this rather than public library work. Training for work with children has no place in such an atmosphere.

There are good libraries, of course, but, as in other countries, they depend greatly on individual enthusiasm and vision. I visited such a library at Himo with Shiego Wanatabe, the Japanese representative on IBBY. Built in 1974, Himo Library was an impressive example of Japanese architecture. It had been planned to preserve as much as possible of the natural beauty of the environment, even to re-locating a shrine. The view from the large windows was of a green space with trees and a stream (in which, a touch of local colour, a woman was washing carrots of an inordinate length). The library was expensively equipped. Birch wood everywhere and a splendidly solid wooden counter in the children's section. The shelves were stocked attractively and there was an eye-catching display of picture books – but there was no children's librarian to encourage the use of these amenities and, although this was a school holiday, not a child was to be seen. However, 50% of the issues were to children and the library was well used by the community. The reason for this was interesting. Originally, it was considered essential to arouse local interest *before* building a library, so a mobile unit was installed first. When this became inadequate to meet the demand, a small branch library was built, confident of local interest and support.

My visit coincided with the 'All Japan Workshop on Children's Literature' at Nagoya, so I was asked to address the delegates. As usual, I was welcomed, with ceremonial bows and many cups of green tea, by the delegation of librarians and city officials (all men). Then, equipped with an extra large bouquet, I was ushered into the hall where 150 delegates awaited me. With the help of my interpreter, I delivered what I hoped was an inspirational, if impromptu, address and then visited each study group. Most of these were painfully serious, but a lighter note was evident in the one concerned with comics for girls. I noticed that these lurid publications were being studied with interest and some hilarity. I also observed that some of them had library labels! I was sorry that my programme did not allow me time to talk with these young people who could have told me so much about children and books. Far too soon, I was being bowed into a car by a phalanx of dignitaries.

However, I did have an opportunity to meet and talk to librarians at the seminar which had been arranged at Hakone, a holiday resort in Isu National Park from which Mount Fuji could be seen - if one was lucky; I only glimpsed it once, insubstantial in the swirling mist. The forty-nine students had been selected from many parts of Japan by means of a questionnaire and an essay. Most of them were from city libraries, a few from rural areas, some were graduates from a library school.

On the first evening I was given an idea of conditions in the many areas from which the students came, a most valuable experience for a foreigner like myself. During the three days of the seminar there were exhaustive sessions on all aspects of library service to children. All these questions were addressed to me and the students seemed to have an implicit faith in my ability to answer them. (I surprised *myself* at what I could answer from experience and specialised knowledge.) I am afraid, however, that my answers were not always as helpful as I could have wished, for conditions were so very different from those in England. However, when translated, my efforts were well received and dutifully inscribed in many notebooks in that complicated script which is written so effortlessly by these skilful calligraphers.

One afternoon, I was excused from attendance as the students needed to think up more questions for me. Their report was presented on a scroll some yards long, with ominous glances at me when there was a particularly demanding question. I was relieved after this ordeal to find that the last session was to be for storytelling. I was intrigued to hear *King John's Christmas* recited in Japanese, and to be able to follow other stories because I knew the original. Then it was my turn. After hearing a resume of my story in their own language, they too were able to follow it in this foreign language – they laughed at the right places anyway! Unexpectedly, they asked if I would read them a poem, so that they might hear "what poetry sounded like in English". I read them Eleanor Farjeon's tender poem *A Bird Calling*, with its musical rhythm. (Eleanor Farjeon is, rather unexpectedly for such a very England writer, well liked in Japan).

This was to be my farewell to the group, now my friends. I signed a copy of my book for each one, and then I took the hand of every student as she bowed. "Come again, Colwell san," they said, many with tears. Here was spontaneous affection for an 'outside person' which touched and humbled me. No longer could I see the 'inscrutable faces' of the East about which I had read in story books!

I gave two public lectures on children's literature and reading tastes. These had been prepared in advance so that my translator, Kyoko, might study them at leisure. It was to be no haphazard affair – with Japanese earnestness we studied each paragraph and practised our 'duet' so that there should be no awkward pauses between speaker and translator.

When we reached the hall where I was to speak, I was amazed to see a long queue waiting. The hall was full, some standing, and two hundred people had been turned away. I heard that a nearby policeman on traffic duty was asked so often for directions to the lecture hall that he became suspicious as to whether this was a seditious meeting. My lecture at Osaka was equally well attended, and was followed by a reception at which I signed a great many copies of my book for librarians from many parts of Japan, including Hokkaido, the northern island, an area where there were no public libraries, only bunko.

To speak with a translator is an odd experience. One must pause in one's train of thought while the translator catches up. When anything amusing is said by the speaker, those who can understand English laugh, the others are unmoved; when the audience hears their native language, they laugh in their turn. The lecturer is a spectator much of the time, dissociated from his or her text, watching its impact.

What of children's books? I am not competent to make an assessment of children's literature in Japan for obvious reasons, the language barrier and the fact that, with the exception of picture-books, so few Japanese books have been translated into English. Folk tales have reached us, too – in fact many of Japanese picture-books use folk tales as a theme. It seems, I am told, that the main trend in fiction books is realism, the realism of a complex modern society concerned with the latest technical inventions.

The publishing output is quite large, and the great proportion of books published are new titles. Book lovers are concerned about this, for it means that the standard books of past times are falling out of print. The reason for this, in part anyway, is said to be the economic pressure exerted by the distributing agencies on whom all publishers depend for the dissemination of their books throughout Japan. These agencies prefer to handle large editions of new books rather than a small number of reprints of the older books.

During my visit I was given the opportunity of meeting a representative group of publishers and editors. This took place in the boardroom of Iwanami Shoten. I was bombarded with questions about the publishing of children's books in England; questions I answered to the best of my ability and, I hope, with some semblance of accuracy. I asked questions, too, about Japan's output and also about publishers' contact with libraries and librarians. It was obvious that the publishers did not consider there would be any advantage in consulting librarians about the reading tastes of their public, children or adults. Librarians had no status in the publishing world. The publishers were astonished to hear of the friendly relations between children's book editors and librarians in the United Kingdom. They were still more surprised to learn that children's book editors met together in a Children's Book Circle for discussion. One editor asked incredulously, "But can editors of rival firms meet? Is it possible without warfare?" I gathered that there was not tacit agreement between editors in Japan about poaching each other's best selling authors.

168

Although so few Japanese books have reached the English market, the traffic the other way was heavy. Looking round library and bookshop shelves, I was impressed by the large number of English and American books to be seen there. Most Carnegie Medal-winning books were translated as a matter of course, and so were the prize books of other countries. The introduction of so many books from the west was due to the vision of Momoko Ishii, who began the translation of the Beatrix Potter books, *Winnie-the-Pooh, The Wind in the Willows* and many others, including Eleanor Farjeon's stories, in the 1950s.

Bookshops are plentiful in Japan and a good proportion specialise in children's books. These are often run by enthusiasts who are genuinely interested in books and children and maintain a high standard of selection. There is an association of booksellers which issues booklists. A number of book prizes have been established by public and private bodies. The number of bookshops of all kinds in Tokyo in the district called Kanda, is large and those I visited were crowded by customers and had a very representative stock.

There are many influences in children's reading in Japan, as in our own country. One is, of course, television. The standard of broadcasting for children was not high. The programmes I saw varied from the silly to the horrific. In the latter, there were two murders and two corpses revived in ghastly detail. The travesties of the classics are later issued as 'The Book of the Television Programme'. Actors adopt an absurdly artificial voice when playing to children. I was told that watching so much television impaired children's powers of concentration so that they were not able to read books of any length. Comics, too, were bought extensively by adults as well as children.

The Japanese system and attitude towards education is relevant here. Education is formal and parents exert exceptional pressure on children to succeed in their studies so as to advance in their future careers. Even children of six must take an examination to pass on to their primary school. Not only do children attend school during the day but, if their parents can afford it, they go to a fee-paying school after school hours as well so as to achieve better examination results. Competition is fierce. By the time young people reach university age, their chances of winning a place there – however hard they have worked – are very limited, for there are many more would-be students than there are vacancies. No wonder some young people crack under the strain of 'Examination Hell'. It is not surprising, too, that, their long day over, children have no energy to do anything but sit passively in front of the television screen.

Many people have said that reading by children is declining. Is this too gloomy a view? The number of Home Libraries is increasing and more children are using public libraries. Individuals who are close to children testify that there *are* book-loving children. The publishers Fukuinkan Shoten who enclose a postcard asking for the reader's opinions in every book they publish, say that they have received many comments from interested children. From experience in our own country, I know that there will always be children for whom books are a necessary part of life and a source of joy and solace. I found Japanese children lively and intelligent, happy children too. My only regret was that I could not speak to the younger ones about the books they enjoyed.

Although of necessity most of my time was taken up by professional interests, my hosts ensured that I should see all that most visitors to Japan enjoy: temples, pagodas and shrines; a fairy tale castle, Himeji, that looked not unlike an iced cake; Japanese gardens with their symbolic patterns of sand and rocks. I endured the diabolical fumes of the Big Hell sulphur springs, and enjoyed the rice fields and the magnificent mountains and forests which cover eighty percent of Japan's territory. On Sunday I joined the holidaying crowds in the Ginza street of Tokyo where, on this one day, all traffic is banned and families picnic happily until, at the stroke of six, cars surge in again. I even experienced a very mild earthquake and realised a little of what it means to feel the solid earth sway beneath one's feet. And everywhere I went there were parades of school children armed with cameras, the boys, known as 'Blackbirds', in their semi-military uniforms, the girls wearing Edwardian sailor blouses and three-quarter length skirts.

I had the good fortune, too, to see something of the arts of Japan. One of these occasions was particularly interesting, a performance of the traditional puppets, Bunraku, seldom seen today. These were life-sized puppets each manipulated by three black-hooded puppeteers who, although they were visible all the time, were unnoticed by the audience. The story was narrated by a professional storyteller, the Taiju, who accompanied his tale on the shamisen, a three-stringed instrument. He used an extraordinary voice, impossible to produce in any natural way, which sounded strangled and was without resonance. At the Kabuki Theatre, there was a most skilful performance in mime by an actor who became a marionette, moving only at the command of non-existent strings.

The most polished performance was at the Kamagawa Theatre, by a company of women - geishas - who combined in a programme of ballet and drama. Their gorgeous costumes, their mask-like faces so devoid of expressions, their stately formal dancing, was perfection. These intelligent women are rigorously trained from an early age in dancing, drama, music and poetry.

I shall not forget the Japanese rooms I occasionally saw. Uncluttered, their only ornament a painted scroll of a flower arrangement in a beautiful vase, the sliding rice-paper screens, the natural wood floors covered with tatami, gave a feeling of harmony and peace unbroken even by a footfall. This, too, was an expression of the art of Japan, a facet of the Japan which, although, it welcomes all that is modern, yet remains at heart a country of tradition.

In 1994, the twentieth Congress of IBBY was hosted by Japan, a further proof of the power of books and a common purpose to bring people of different nations together in friendly discussion. The award was made to a Japanese poet for children. The poems were later translated into English by the Empress of Japan.

This then, was Japan for me – and unforgettable country of unfamiliar sights and sounds quite unlike anything I had known previously. This was the gift my Japanese friends gave me, a gift of warm friendship which wiped out for ever my preconceived ideas about their country. I am grateful that I am still remembered there after so many years.

A LAST WORD

I was born in the 'Edwardian summer' of 1904, a period when English society was still only just emerging from the Victorian standards and way of life. My childhood was a far cry from that of children of today, for radio was in its infancy and the tyranny of television undreamt of. There were few motor vehicles, and aviation was still in the experimental stage. Yet children had one aspect denied to the over-protected children of today: a freedom to find one's own adventures, to invent one's own games, to be independent in a countryside that was still largely unspoilt.

Looking down the vista of my long life of 95 years, I begin to see a pattern emerging, a way of life which brought me diversity of experience and a richness of friendship which has been my joy and support.

The greatest gift that life has given me is my many friends in all parts of the world, especially those pioneers in my library- and book-world. Working with these women has brought me to places I would never have experienced, like the USA, Canada, Scandinavia and Europe. In recent years, the revival of storytelling has introduced me to many new friends. I am indeed blessed, for everyone needs to love and be loved.

In 1992, I became partially sighted due to a condition known as molecular degeneration. I can no longer read the printed word, nor see the faces of my friends. Nor can I see the red on the robin's breast or the ladybird on the heather. However, I am grateful that I am not blind and can still enjoy the sight of scudding white clouds overhead in the 'blue ethereal sky'.

In 1993, my sister, Vera, died after a long and distressing illness. We had always been close, for we were much of an age, and our brother and sister were already teenagers when we were born.

My retirement to Loughborough in 1967 enabled us to join forces for several years of peaceful happiness together. Vera had her garden, music and painting, I had my books and storytelling.

Now this happy time was over, but I was fortunate indeed in the affection of my three nieces and nephew, who although they lived respectively in the USA, France, Scotland and England, maintained their loving care of me.

Now that I am coming to the last chapter of the long story which is my life, I am grateful for all that is past and trust for all that is to come.

APPENDIX

Text of the Woodfield Lecture VIII
given by Eileen Colwell, MBE, D.Litt.,
at the Department of Library and Information Studies,
Loughborough University, 1985

THE CHILD AND HIS BOOK

Random reflections

All my life I have been happily involved with books and children and, as a Children's Librarian, I have had the privilege and opportunity of observing the meeting between them. As all librarians know, this can be both an exciting and a disconcerting experience, for an adult's conception of what a child will enjoy does not necessarily coincide with that of the child.

A child's ability to appreciate a variety of books and authors depends considerably on what is available to him. Looking back at my own childhood, I realise that much of what I read would be considered as beyond my age, but I am sure I was not unusual in this at that period. I had little opportunity to read children's books for I had access to very few. Once – what pleasure! – we were given a bound volume of *The Strand* magazine and there I met E. Nesbit and Sherlock Holmes for the first time, but my chief source of books was my father's extensive library. There I discovered for myself Dickens, Scott, Thackeray, the Brontës, R. L. Stevenson and many other so-called 'Classics'. To me they were not 'required reading', boring, difficult books, but just stories. I have been grateful ever since that I discovered something of English literature so early in life.

Why didn't I use a library as a source of books? Because there were no libraries in the small provincial towns in which we lived. As for a children's department, such a waste of the library rate was almost unheard of. Once only did I encounter a library and it was such a forbidding experience that I didn't repeat it for many years. It was on the indicator system and borrowers had to ask for books by catalogue numbers. The librarian terrified me – he was old with a walrus moustache and eyebrows to rival those of Edward Blishen. He seemed to consider my requests for stories as a personal affront and at last, irritated beyond endurance, he picked up a book at random, stamped it and slammed it down before me. I seized it and escaped. Only when I got home did I discover it to be Mrs. Henry Wood's story *Mrs. Haliburton's Troubles*, the trials of a clergyman's wife. I was *ten* years old at the time! Could it be that this rejection of a child's longing for books later developed into my dream that – some day – I would have a library where children would be welcome to browse at will amongst books especially chosen for them? Wonderfully fortunate, I realised that dream to the full before I was twenty-five, at a time when children's libraries were almost non-existent. But that is another story...

And so began my long and happy experience of children and books. I soon discovered that there are three kinds of readers; the children who will tackle any kind of book because they are natural and compulsive readers. These will welcome suggestions of new authors to try. At the other extreme are the boys and girls who have no use for books and feel that reading has no relevance to their lives. Quite often this group lack reading skills also, an added factor. Today television has claimed these children and helps them with its visual presentation. In between these two groups is a third group of children who can read fluently enough, can recognise the value of books as a source of information, but who read unadventurously. They have drifted into a rut of favourite authors, often undemanding, and are unaware of the books they *might* enjoy. This is the group that offers a challenge to librarians. Provided one knows one's borrowers and a wide range of books, it is sometimes possible to obey the old adage and 'give the right book to the right child at the right time'. It is worth a try and a test of the librarian's ability and sensitiveness. This expertise and personal interest in a child's reading is the quality I find lacking in some libraries today where, for various reasons, the staff has little opportunity to spend time with individual children, or where the 'open plan' precludes the privacy and personal relationships that children enjoy. Children should be able to have confidence in their librarian's knowledge of the books and the shelves. The excellent provision for children to follow their own interests in many libraries today cannot take the place of a friendly adult who has time to listen and help. There is a danger that special activities may crowd out reading altogether. I remember a library in Denmark where children were busily playing with games and gadgets – *one* child only was reading with his fingers in his ears. I am aware that the conception of the purpose of a library has changed, but is this really progress?

Does it matter what a child reads as long as he goes through the action of reading? I am often challenged on this by teachers. Of course it matters what children do with the skill they have acquired so painfully. Childhood is so brief and, sadly, growing briefer every year, and the counter-attractions to reading are so many, that the first acquaintance with books should be not only enjoyable but worth-while.

I am often asked to define what makes a 'good book', an impossible task. I am not thinking at the moment of factual books which explore the rational world and answer everyday questions, but of those books called 'fiction', those imaginative stories which are concerned with the other equally important side of our natures. Alison Uttley described imagination as 'the power of seeing the invisible, of bringing forth that essence of beauty or pure enchantment that lies hidden within each object...' In our modern materialistic world concerned chiefly with making money and what it can buy, we need the 'Music-makers and the dreamers of dreams' more than ever.

But what *does* distinguish one book from another, what is the difference between a run-of-the-mill book produced to 'cash in' on the market and a book which is memorable, can be read more than once and has a quality and originality peculiarly its own? De la Mere said 'Writing for children will need every virtue, every grace that is aspired to by the artist in fiction'. 'A good children's book,' says Geoffrey Trease, 'is one that uses language skilfully to entertain, to stimulate imagination, to represent reality and to communicate ideas.' William Mayne says, 'A children's book can be of the simplest, but possess drama, thought, vocabulary.' We cannot adequately define a 'good book' – it differs for every child – but we can perhaps claim the right to expect that the writer will select, create, make patterns, put together certain characters and events in such a way as to produce an absorbing story which illuminates an aspect of life for the reader.

An absorbing story – this is the prime essential for children's enjoyment. Children of every generation have demanded stories as their right, not always written for them, sometimes annexed as, for example, *Robinson Crusoe*. Children still want to *hear* stories, a desire often neglected in these days of working mothers, disturbed family life and the ubiquitous television with its flashing lights and continuous noise. Live storytelling has almost disappeared – although there are signs of a

175

revival of interest in the spoken word. Teachers *read* to children but seldom *tell* them a story. But I find in my travels about Britain that children *do* want to listen to stories and lose themselves in them, reflecting excitement, sadness and laughter unreservedly.

All stories are escapist to some degree – why else do adults read so many thrillers and 'Barbara Cartlands'! Girls used to lose themselves in school stories – ah, those midnight feasts and secret passages and exiled princesses! Boys escaped for a glorious hour with Biggles and Western stories. What matters is *what else*, other than escapist, stories are, what extra dimension do they add for the child? So, a first escape for children is into fairy tales and fantasy where there are 'perilous seas and fairy lands forlorn', journeys and quests, happy endings. No matter that the diarist, John Aubrey, asserted that 'The last fairy disappeared in the seventeenth century with a delicious perfume and a most melodious twang'. The tinsel fairy at the top if the Christmas tree may be derided today, but *magic* stills delights. In spite of the countless marvellous discoveries – unknown in my childhood – now commonplace, a child can still feel wonder, can still believe 'as many as three impossible things before breakfast', leap spontaneously from one possibility to another. Hence the acceptance of such a place as Masefield's Witch's Cupboard with its flask of 'Invisible Mixture' and ivory box labelled 'Ointment for turning little boys into Tom-tits'. Accepted, too is C. S. Lewis' country of Narnia through the wardrobe, or the lands of the Hobbits, or de la Mare's Tishnar, 'the endless unknown'.

No book can be called a 'good book' unless it shows the reader three-dimensional characters, people who seem so real that he suffers with them when they are in trouble, rejoices when they are rescued and 'live happily ever after'. I remember reading an anecdote about Samuel Richardson's *Pamela*, a book which, incidentally, 'was designed to cultivate the principles of virtue and religion'! It was published in parts and in one village, the blacksmith read these aloud to his neighbours. When Pamela, that greatly tried young lady, at last married the man she loved, the villagers ran to church and rang the bells for joy! Children can feel involved like this with characters in books. '*Black Beauty* is heart-warming and sorrowful. I cried when Ginger died'...'I like this family (*Little Women*) because the people are real and you can imagine you are living with them'...and this from a boy of eight rather pathetically 'I like Brer Rabbit because he laughs at Brer Fox although he has troubles. I wish I could do the same...' And the villains – 'Long John Silver is smashing, he's a *proper* pirate'; or Margaret Mahy's sinister Mr. Braque;

Lucy Boston's spine-chilling yew-tree, Noah, 'that clutches at the air with long fingers' and advances inexorably with 'the sound of dragging and brushing of twigs'...

Can *you* remember what it was like to fall under the spell of a book? Thoughts cease to wander, attention becomes concentration, absorption, surrender, and we are in another world, a world of imagination that knows no bounds. Everyone here, I suspect, could bring to mind characters from the books they read as children – Alice and the Cheshire Cat, Paddington and his marmalade sandwiches, Tom Sawyer and Huck Finn, even Peter Rabbit and Jemima Puddleduck. Sadly the character of the astringent Mary Poppins has become identified with Julie Andrews with her charm and her singing, the homely Doctor Dolittle is now a rather uneasy Rex Harrison and Mowgli has been taken over by the cartoon world with wise old Bagheera and Shere Khan mere travesties of themselves.

Ultimately the characters an author creates depend on what he is himself or herself. Almost insensibly characters reflect the author's own attitude to life, his experiences, his beliefs and so have the ring of truth.

The setting of a children's story is important because it adds verisimilitude, whether the story is of a real place or an imaginary one. Many a boy or girl has explored Arthur Ransome's landscape or Watership Down, book in hand. A reader can walk about in Cynthia Harnett's or Leon Garfield's London with confidence. Laura Ingalls Wilder's pioneer stories ring true always – listen to this:

> The dim wagon track went no further in the prairie and Pa stopped the horses. When the wagon wheels stopped turning, Jack [the family dog] dropped down in the shade between them. His belly sank on the grass and his front legs stretched out. His nose fitted into the furry hollow. All of him rested except his ears.

And here is Charles Kingsley, whose versions of the Greek stories are still unsurpassed:

> He came to the land of everlasting night where the air was full of feathers and the soil was hard with ice; and there at last he found the Three Grey Sisters by the shores of the freezing sea, nodding upon a white log of driftwood beneath the cold white winter moon...

The touchstone that sets the seal upon what we consider to be an outstanding book, is style. What is style? Again it is impossible to

define, except loosely as the way in which an author uses words. Ezra
Pound said in *How to Read*, 'Great literature is simply language charged
with meaning to the utmost degree'. Surely this is particularly true of
children's literature for nowhere else must an author use words so spar-
ingly. Because of the necessary strictures in length in a children's book,
there is no room for 'purple passages'. Only the most direct words will
do, the *right* words. It is an author's idiosyncratic style that makes
'words walk up and down in the hearts of the hearers'. Big words for
little matters have no particular value, a plethora of words adds nothing
for the child if *one* will do. (I am reminded of the dreadful examples we
hear every day – 'In this day and age'...'Children in a learning situation'...the gobbledegook which is used to give weight to a commonplace situation, the jargon, the constant use of 'Ye'know'.)

Childhood is the time when the magic of words can be absorbed
almost unconsciously. A child is a baffling mixture of receptivity and
inattention to the waves of words that break over him, words which,
even if only half understood, have a mysterious charm and please the
ear with the rhythm of their sounds. Hence the attraction to all children
of Lear's 'The owl and the pussycat went to sea...'

Do children appreciate words? I think they do. Listen to a child of
nine on the subject:

> *The boring words ...*
> *I look at them dragging their feet*
> *But when the exciting, marvellous words*
> *Jump out, I dance and sing with them.*
> *The boring, the dreary words*
> *Slip back into the book. Good for them!*
> *I like the words that liven me up!*

There is a tendency nowadays to simplify language for children, a
form of condescension, for most children are quite capable of understanding a word *in its context*, as part of a sentence. Who can doubt for
instance what Mrs. Tabitha Twitchett means when, as she smacks Tom
Kitten, she says 'I am affronted!' A young Yorkshire boy, asked if he
understood the word 'Exhausted', looked at the picture of Jemima
Puddleduck toiling up the hill and answered 'Aye – puffed!' Few children nowadays can read books my own generation read with ease, to be
fair, neither can I understand computer jargon, but this is no excuse for
abridging adult classics so that children may read them. Insight into

human nature learnt from experience, the author's individual style, passages of description, are ruthlessly swept away on the pretext that they slow down the action. With them goes much of the warmth and life and genius of the author's original. What remains is a story perhaps – not always a good one when reduced to its bare bones – but not the book the author wrote. 'Potted versions' in childhood too often mean that the reader never reads the original. Even books for *children* are tampered with. Recently Masefield's *The Midnight Folk* and *A Box of Delights* have been abridged unnecessarily and *The Wind in the Willows* has suffered several times. Why not leave the child to do his own abridging by the age-old device of skipping those parts for which he is not yet ready.

There is one last dimension of a good book, the most important of all. Story-content, characters, setting and style, all these are as nothing if a book does not make us *feel* – beauty, laughter, joy and sorrow. Cold, clinical stories written to order or to 'fill a gap' are ephemeral and do not move us. It is the books written from the heart, from passionate conviction, that light up the imagination and are remembered. Such 'shining moments' are re-created from a personal experience, perhaps of beauty as in Jane Gardam's remembrance of a frozen waterfall in her book *The Hollow Land*.

> *And there stood high as the sky, a chandelier of icicles. Hundreds and hundreds of them down the shale steps of a waterfall...And not only water had turned to spears of glass but every living thing about – the grasses, the rushes, the spiders' webs, the great tall fearless thistles. And as the sun reached them they all turned at once to every colour known...*

Or that moment of ecstasy in Alan Garner's *The Stone Book* when Mary climbs with her father, a stonemason, to the church spire and for a few glorious seconds rides the weathercock high above the world:

> *Her bonnet fell off and hung by its ribbons, and the wind filled her hair. 'Faster! Faster!' she shouted. 'I'm not frit!' She banged her heels on the golden sides and the weathercock boomed.*
> *Father let the spike stop and lifted her down. 'There,' he said, 'You'll remember this day, my girl, for the rest of your life.'*
> *'I already have,' said Mary.*

Let us not forget the value of laughter, for it is natural for children to want to laugh, although their sense of humour is more slapstick than subtle – the appreciation of wit comes later. It is not easy to write humorous books, it is a gift given to few. J. B. S. Haldane, the eminent scientist, had it and his book *My Friend, Mr. Leakey*, has given generations of children pleasure. How nice to know a man who has an octopus as a servant and a small dragon who lives in the heart of a fire, but puts on asbestos boots when he steps on the carpet! Then there is Helen Cresswell's *The Pie Makers* and the saga of the appalling Bagthorpes. Recently a real comic genius has appeared for children, Dick King-Smith, whose ridiculous story of *The Sheep-Pig* won the Whitbread prize. I recommend it to adults too!

But for most of us, adults or children, it is the books that touch our hearts that become part of us and which we remember for years. Not the excessively emotional stories of the Victorian era with their chronically weeping heroines and untimely death-beds – does anyone here remember *The Wide, Wide World* or *Misunderstood*, I wonder? It is real life situations that children can share that moves them, sometimes to tears. This is why Mrs. Hodgson Burnett's *The Secret Garden* is still enjoyed although it was written nearly fifty years ago. There is a poignant moment in Philippa Pearce's *Tom's Midnight Garden* that many children remember, when Tom says to Hatty in the garden that no longer exists in the present:

> 'You're a ghost and I've proved it. You're dead and gone and a ghost!'
> There was a quietness, then, in which could be heard a cuckoo's stuttering cry from the woods beyond the garden; and then the sound of Hatty's beginning softly to weep.
> 'I'm not dead – oh, please, Tom, I'm not dead'

I have never known a group of children hearing the story of Sohrab and Rustem for the first time, fail to be moved by its tragic end. Can anyone read the final paragraph of Henry Williamson's *Tarka the Otter* without sadness and shame for man's inhumanity:

> Below the island the river widened, smooth with the sky. Tarka swam down slowly, bleeding from many wounds...At the beginning of the tenth hour he passed the banks faced with stone to keep the sea from the village and drifted into deeper waters...Hounds were called off by the horn for the tide was at the flood. But as they were about to leave, Tarka was seen again, moving with the tide.
> And the tide slowed still, and began to move back, and they waited and

watched...and while they stood there silently, a great bubble rose out of the depths and broke, and as they watched, another bubble shook to the surface and broke; and there was a third bubble on the sea-going waters, and nothing more.

It is in books like these – and many others known to those who read children's literature – that a child grows up and forgets his own small concerns in a wider view. To live in imaginative stories is to be open to new ideas and impressions beyond the immediate, to learn tolerance, compassion, understanding.

Let me conclude with a few comments on some aspects of the world of children's literature today. No longer can children's books be dismissed as 'only for the kids'. Children's literature is an integral part of the main stream of literature and is rich in interest and fine and imaginative writing.

Reading is still a personal activity in which a child can find his own level and follow his own taste *at his own pace*, in spite of the pressures of the media and educational theories. The themes of all stories, whether for adults or children, are still what they have always been – divided loyalties, hate and love, the dilemma of right and wrong in a changing society, the need for a greater power than ourselves. Isaac Bashevis Singer has said that adult authors choose to move into the field of children's books 'because they see there a last refuge from a literature for adults gone berserk and ready for suicide'. Let us hope that children's books do not go the same way in the anxiety of some authors to show the futility of the modern world as they see it, a place of cynicism and despair. We have no right to force the negation of hope on the future generation. There are areas of moral and emotional experience which should be left until young people are ready to face them.

Although personal ownership of books by children is much more possible today because of the ubiquitous paperback, libraries are still the main source of books for the young. Unhappily the widespread cuts in library incomes and the resulting shortage of staff and books are having an adverse effect upon children too. Yet this is the generation which will have more leisure than ever before and will need what books can offer, food for the imagination and the mind.

The publishing of children's books while still 'a staggering strength of scribblings' flood', as a Bulgarian librarian described it to me, is affected today by the current business tycoons who take over a variety of firms, which may well include a publishing company, with no interest except in the resulting financial gain. Fortunately we have dedicated children's book editors who still manage to maintain a standard in spite of the demands made upon them. I have faith in our British children's books and I believe we have every right to be proud of our authors and illustrators. Wherever I have travelled in Europe, the States or the East, I have found familiar names on the shelves in bookshops.

In the field of criticism and children's literature as a whole, I often feel that we are becoming too serious and specialised. The pendulum has swung too far from the original disregard of children's books as literature. Today children's books are analysed and dissected, are the subject of university theses, seminars, workshops and conferences. Authors – usually those who are deceased and so cannot defend themselves – are psychoanalysed and 'debunked'. Kenneth Grahame, Lewis Carroll and even Arthur Ransome, are accused of 'something nasty in the woodshed'. Only a few weeks ago an author, Humphrey Carpenter, in *Secret Gardens*, has argued that what Lewis Carroll was really doing in *Alice in Wonderland* was 'to create something that is specifically a mockery of Christian belief' and that *Peter Pan* is 'an alternative religion'. Shades of the Mad Hatter and the Cheshire Cat! Are we, in studying children's literature in this way, in danger of losing sight of the children for whom it is intended? Are we forgetting that the boys and girls who read children's books are individuals who cannot be classified arbitrarily and who read primarily for enjoyment?

Pessimists foretell the death of books – and even words – in our extraordinary technological age. What would our world be like then, asks the poet, Louis MacNeice:

> When books have all seized up like the books in graveyards
> And reading and even speaking have been replaced
> By other, less difficult, media, we wonder if you
> Will find in flowers and fruit the same colour and taste
> They held for those for whom they were framed in words.
> And will your grass be green, your sky be blue,
> Or will your birds be always wingless birds.

That day has not come yet. It is still our responsibility and pleasure to ensure that this generation of children, vulnerable and threatened so direly by the pressures of modern life, have, as their right, access to the best books available. Technological and social conditions may change radically, but the fundamental values endure, and, as de la Mare said, 'Only the best is good enough for children'.

BOOKS BY EILEEN COLWELL

How I became a Librarian 1956 (Nelson)
    Japanese Edition 1968 - Fukuinkan Shoten
    Japanese Edition 1974 - JLA
    Japanese Edition 1994 - Koguma Publishing Co

Eleanor Farjeon 1961 Bodley Head; Japanese Edition 1988 -
    Shindokusho - sha
Eleanor Farjeon 1962 (American Edition)
Tell me a Story 1962 Penguin
A Storyteller's Choice 1963 Bodley Head; American Edition 1964
Tell me Another Story 1964 Puffin
A Second Storyteller's Choice 1965 Bodley Head
A Halloween Acorn 1966 Bodley Head
Time for a Story 1967 Bodley Head
The Youngest Story Book 1967 Bodley Head
First Choice 1968 LA A basic book list for children
Princess Splendour and Other Stories 1969 Longman
Bad boys: A Collection of Stories 1972 Longman
Round about and long ago: Folk tales from the counties of England
    1972 Longman; also published in Japan
Tales from the Islands: Round the Coast of Britain 1975 Kestral;
    also published in Japan
Little Greyneck (Text re-written - a picture-book - a Russian Folktale)
    Kestral (Eng. Ed); Kestral (Russian Ed)
The Magic Umbrella and Other Stories for Telling 1976 Bodley Head
Eileen Colwell Koenroku: Books and Children
    1976 Tokyo Kodomo toshokan
Humblepuppy and Other Stories for Telling 1978 Bodley Head
The Lost Land and Other Stories 1979 Rockets
The Devil's Bridge and Other Stories 1979 Rockets
More Stories to Tell 1979 Puffin
Storytelling 1980 Bodley Head; 2nd Edition 1991 Thimble Press;
    Japanese Edition - 1995 Koguma Publishing
Bedtime Stories 1982 Ladybird
Highdays and Holidays 1988 Viking Kestrel; 1989 Puffin
Cats in a Basket 1993 Viking
Wagging Tales 1993 Viking

List of names of the subscribers for ONCE UPON A TIME

Kimiko Abe
Marianne Adey
Aldbourne Children's
  Book Group
Shizuko Anada
Janet Andrew
Mihoko Arai
Tokuko Arai
Mikiko Araki
Mineko Arata
Kazuko Asami
Kumiko Asaoka
Etsuko Ashida
Clive Barnes
Sue Bates
Nina Bawden
Lois Beeson
Elizabeth Bellwood
Jenny & David Blanch
Constance Boyle
Theresa Breslin
Chris Brown
Mrs M Bruÿn
Aidan Chambers
The Cherwell School
Children's Bookshop,
  Huddersfield
Patricia Crampton
June Crebbin
Helen Cresswell
Olive Crouch
Barry Cunningham
Kiyoko Date
Julia Donaldson
Penny Dolan
Katy Dunn née Boyton
John Dunne
Rowena Edlin-White
Keiko Enosawa
Dr Philip W Errington
Mrs Halcyon Evans
Professor Margaret
  Evans

Jane Everson
Bea Ferguson
Lindsey Fraser
Sanae Fujii
Yoriko Fujikura
Takako Fujiwara
Yoko Fukai
Yoko Fukuda
Keiko Fukukawa
Yumiko Fukumoto
Chiaki Furukado
Mrs D Margaret Garratt
Prue Goodwin
Anne Gorman
Michael Gorman
Alison Grant
Grace Hallworth
Naomi Haraguchi
Keiko Harikae
Anne Harvey
  & Gervase Farjeon
Hisako Hashimoto
Elizabeth Hawkins
Antony Hemming
Toyomi Hidaka
Chise Higashibaba
Mieko Hirata
Anna Home
Mrs Judy Taylor Hough
Mrs P A Howard
Audrey Hutchison
Fiona Hunt
Keiko Ibaraki
Miyoko Ichikawa
Sanae Ichikawa
Tae Ichikawa
Mamiko Ihara
Mahoko Iino
Kazuko Ikeda
Noriko Imaizumi
Rose Impey
Tomoko Irii
Elizabeth Irwin-Hunt

Haruko Ishikawa
Michiko Ishikawa
Mari Isoda
Sumiko Isokawa
Ikuko Ito
Kinuyo Iwahori
Natsuko Iwata
Susie Jenkin-Pearce
Mrs Ursula John
Kazuko Kato
Setsuko Kato
Yuko Kitagawa
Yukako Kitamura
Gishin Kobayashi
Izumi Kobayashi
Atsuko Kubo
Kayoko Kuratsu
Akiko Kurita
Mary Leake
Robert Leeson
Primrose Lockwood
Pat McPherson
Patrick T McSharry
Sheila Madders
Kayoko Maeda
Yvonne Manning
Jan Mark
Rita Marks
The John Masefield
  Society
Mr E R Mason
Beverley Mathias
Kyoko Matsuoka
Mari Matsumura
Mary Medlicott
Margaret Meek
Michi Mimoto
Yumiko Mitsudo
Hiroko Mochizuki
Mrs Annie Moerkercken
Monmouthshire
  Libraries
Pat Moon

Manami Morimoto
Nobuko Morio
Miss Diana J Morrell
Robin Morrow
Elaine Moss
Kyoko Murakawa
Yasuko Nagaso
Naoko Naito
Toshiko Nakai
Sachi Nakao
Elizabeth Goodway
   Napier
North Birmingham
Children's Book Group
Northamptonshire
Libraries & Info. Service
Miss Jayne O'Brien
Michiko Ogata
Haruka Ohashi
Reiko Ohno
Ritsuko Ohnuki
Yutaka Oishi
Shuichi Omori
Miyuri Onishi
Michiyo Ono
Gwen Orwin
   née Hutchinson
Katsumi Otsuka
Keiko Ozama
Susette Palmer
W Roy Pape
Eileen Parnwell
Mrs K Pascall
The Patuel Family
Bette Paul
Margaret Payne
Philippa Pearce
Joan M Phillips
Ann Pilling
Caroline Pitcher
Jane Ray
Sheila Ray

Diana Rogers
Norimi S.
Judith St. John
Tomoko Sakakibara
Mrs G Salway
Jan Sanderson
Hidekazu Sato
Miiko Sato
Yuko Sekiya
Kyoko Shiba
Harumi Shibata
Yoko Shibata
Izumi Shimahara
Junko Shimizu
Masako Shimizu
Chikako Shimoyama
Sachie Shinohara
Junko Shiozaki
Yoshiko Shiraiwa
Emily Smith
Yung Suk Song
Solihull Children's
   Book Group
South Birmingham
Children's Book Group
Mary Steele
Enid & Chris Stephenson
Kazuko Sudo
Hiroko Sugawara
Midori Suzuki
Bob & Brenda Swindells
Yoko Taguchi
Taeko Tajima
Seiko Takaishi
Pat Tate
Mrs Theta Taylor
Mrs J H Thomas
Pat Thomson
Gillian & Jeanine Thorpe
Ann Thwaite
Yoko Tochiya
Haruko Tokunaga

Keiko Tominaga
Tsumura Central Library,
   City of Nagoya
Atsumi Tsutsui
Nicholas Tucker
Mrs Judith M S Turner
Akiyo Ujiie
Sonoko Uno
Bob Vaughan
Jill Paton Walsh
   & John Rowe Townsend
Shigeo Watanabe
Liz Weir
Kathryn White
Rosemary Wilkie
Mrs Ursula Moray
   Williams
Mr Michael J Wills
Isabel Wilner
Barbara Wilson
   née Roberts
June Wilson
Anne Wood
Kit Wright
Norman B Wrigley
Stephen A Wrigley
Tomiko Yamada
Reiko Yamaguchi
Makiko Yamamoto
Chieko Yamazaki
Hiroko Yamazaki
Haruyo Yanagisawa
Hiromi Yasukawa
Setsuko Yokoyama
Yushie Yokoyama
Yasufumi Yoshii
Noriko Yoshikawa
Yoko Yoshino
Yukie Yotsuda
Yuzawa
Ed Zaghini

OTHER BOOKS FROM PENNINE PENS.

PUBLISHED AUTUMN, 2000

Animal Antics, a collection of children's poems by Debjani Chatterjee.
(1 873378 03 3)

The Redlit Boys, a collection of poems by William Bedford
(1 873378 87 4)

Email from the Provinces, a collection of poems by Simon Fletcher
(1 873378 63 7)

OTHERS

A Little Bridge, a collection of poems by Debjani Chatterjee, Basir Kazmi and Simon Fletcher. These three talented Northern poets have collaborated in a collection of poems which reflects the connections between the cultures of Britain and the Indian sub-continent.   (1 873378 77 7)

The Occasions of Love, a collection of love poems by Simon Fletcher
(1 873378 07 6)

The Chess Board, a play by Basir Kazmi (1 873378 27 0)

Sylvia Plath: Killing the Angel in the House (2nd edition) by Elaine Connell, A very readable introduction to the works of this great poet. (1 873378 01 7) Elaine Connell also maintains the **Sylvia Plath Forum** - www.sylviaplathforum.com

View from the Bridge, (1 873378 47 5) **Back to the Bridge** (1 873378 52 1) and **A Bridge Too Far** (1 873378 57 2) - satirical sketches of life in a small Pennine milltown from John Morrison.

Presenting the Past: Anne Lister of Halifax by Jill Liddington
(1 873378 02 5)

Me, Mick and M31 by Andrew Bibby (1 873378 12 2)
Children's environmental mystery

Cycling in Search of the Cathars by Chris Ratcliffe and Elaine Connell
CD-rom version of book now available

More details of Pennine Pens publications
and web design at the Pennine Pens website
www.penninepens.co.uk